BREATHE AGAIN

BREATHE AGAIN

BREATHE AGAIN

VOL. I

Compiled By:
Trena D. Stephenson

Publisher:
Daughters of Distinction

"BREATHE AGAIN" Series Vol I
Published by Daughters of Distinction

Baltimore MD 21215 USA

Copyright © 2019 DOFDLLC
Daughters Of Distiniction

All rights reserved. No part of the book may be reproduced in any form without permission in writing from the publisher, except in the case of brief quotations embodied in articles or reviews

Cover Design and Layout: Ebony Richardson
Editorial: Dr. Mia G. McGee

Acknowledgements

With Many Thanks

I would like to thank God for being my creator and my all-in all. To my beautiful daughter who I love dearly, thanks for the love and support you give continually. To my parents, my aunt Elder Regina Holmes and my extended family, thanks for being there when I needed you the most. To WofGod Inc. staff and affiliates, thanks so much for all you do to hold my arms up. I could not do what I do without you. To my Daughters of Distinction staff, you all rock! Thanks for all you do. Now we can breathe a little, but do not get too comfortable though. The ride is just beginning. To My Pastor William Powell and Apostle Dr. Yolanda Powell of Dominion International Ministries., thanks for being such an awesome covering for my ministry team and me. I love you both very much. To the awesome vessel of God who did the foreword of this book, My Apostle Dr. Yolanda Powell, your contribution to this project is greatly appreciated. Finally, yet importantly, thanks to all my co-authors of this book. I am so Godly proud of you. The best is yet to come for every one of you. God stretched us and made us better vessels of honor for His sake. If I have forgotten anyone, charge my head and not my heart. Thank you, thank you, and thank you.

With Love
Trena

Foreword

"...then the Lord God formed [that is, created the body of] man from the dust of the ground, and breathed into his nostrils the breath of life; and the man became a living being [an individual complete in body and spirit]." Genesis 2:27 (AMP)

God created man with the breath of life…His very own life, that man might have "a spiritual life" as a kind of resource and receptacle to receive God who is Spirit. What a tremendous gift! Breathe is truly the Father's greatest gift to Mankind. It was so paternal, loving and life-giving for the Lord God Almighty to intimately impart His own 'breathing wind' into His sons and daughters—so that we might live in eternal connection to Him…each an everyday of our lives. His breath then is a perpetual reminder that we came from Him and belong to Him!

Genesis 2:7 says that when the breath of life was breathed into the nostrils of the body of man, man became a living soul. God used two kinds of materials—the dust for making man's body and the breath of life for producing man's spirit. When these two things came together, right away man became a living being. Yes, breath is what connects us to the Father and reminds us daily of His Everlasting Love. We are His finest creation and we reflective Him as we breathe in air and expel it with great rejoicing!

Every day and throughout the extent of our lives we are on an automated, God-designed breathing system that pumps air into our lungs and then expels it, in loving rhythm. How awesome.

Yet, life has a way of attempting to "take our breath" and hinder our ability to oxygenate and resuscitate our inner being. When conflict, confusion or chaos comes…we often "hold our breath." It's often unconscious and unknown to us. But, in such times we must learn to release the life that God placed within us. We must learn to Breathe Again!

In this rich and robust anthology, you will hear author after author and read story after story of how to do just that! How to Breathe Again after the trials, transitions or traumas that often accompany life on this planet. There are healing waters and second winds in these pages. It is a living book of God's breath, released lovingly through His people. So, take the time to inhale and exhale with each chapter. My apostolic daughter and our lead author Apostle Trena Stephenson, knows how to resuscitate the hurting and bring "ruach" wind to the Body of Christ. We all salute her in this literary journey and know that you will be thoroughly blessed as you embrace the critical moment of choosing life, choosing wealth, choosing wholeness…and choosing to Breathe Again!

With Joy Unspeakable & Full of Glory!

Apostle, Dr. Yolanda Powell

Lead Visionary
Dominion's Prophetic & Apostolic
Coalition Transcontinental (D'PACT)
Washington, DC

Table of Contents

Breathing Is Not Always Easy 13

One Last Breath 21

Finding Time To Pray 29

The Secret to the Presence of God 37

Gods Change Agents 45

Come Up Out of the Ashes 55

I Am Persuaded 63

Stolen Breaths 69

Forgive Again 75

I Was In The Dark 85

Once I Was Able to Exhale 95

Breathe Again 103

JUNIA ARISE 113
Bonus Chapter

Daughters of Distinction

Chapter 1

Breathing Is Not Always Easy

10 But he knoweth the way that I take: when he hath tried me, I shall come forth as gold."(Job 23:10 – KJV)

I was excited to be a chosen vessel for this assignment. I thought long and hard naturally/spiritually about what to write. I didn't just want to write anything, but I wanted something that would bless you spiritually, mentally and physically. I needed God to speak to the whole person not just to the carnal man. It was important and imperative not only for you to "Breathe Again", but for me to explain the process of breathing. I correlate the word breathing with living. Therefore, if you want to breathe again to me as a prophetic insight it means to live again. As we look at the word again it actually means either to do over or try it a second time. This means that somewhere along the lines of life there were some issues. These issues could have been good or bad. However, it went; it caused you to stop breathing or shall I say it hindered your life in some way. Sometimes, when walking through this road called life we stumble across bad seasons, unexpected and unforeseen circumstances. These kinds of circumstances can take the life right out of you and cause you to stop breathing. Once your life has been shattered it is not always easy to recover. So, for that reason, I named this chapter "Breathing is Not

Always Easy."

What exactly do I mean by that? As I said before, I correlate breathing with living. If and when you live long enough you will come across sickness, pain, betrayal, destruction and even death. Then, reality sets in that life is not always easy. It is one thing to see it exist in the world, but it's another thing when it hits your front door and enters your home. I was led to write this from a personal perspective because I know what it feels like to be broken, betrayed and yet, healed and restored. I know what it feels like to serve God and not get my prayers answered. To wonder where God is in the hour when I most need Him. Why did God allow this to happen to me? Where are you God and why won't you answer? I always believed that if I served God He would not let anything bad happen to me. I was led to believe that once I got saved it was smooth sailing and everything was going to be perfect. That life would be great and all things would work out good. Well, that was the furthest thing from the truth. So I'm writing this to help all those who believe this and who will ultimately be blindsided just as I was. That was what I considered my eye opening stage. For, truly I lacked knowledge, truth and walked in spiritual immaturity. We all walk in it at some point and it can be devastating. Why? Because I struggled with what I heard (people) rather then what I knew (Truth/Bible).

For many years, I sat in church hearing the preached word; but not having any real revelation. I went by what I heard and saw because I had not taken control of my own spiritual life. I walked in tradition or should I say religion instead of relationship, which was fine because life was great and all things were working out for my good. I was in the prime of my life and was living my dream when all of a sudden tragedy struck. In the blink of an eye, I went from living to barely breathing to fighting for my life. Wow! Now, the day had come when I could no longer rely on people or religion. I had to rely on my faith and God's Word. Which I thought I had very little of. It was testing time and the wind had been knocked right out of me. Where do I go from here? Oh, Lord now what do I do? I can't help myself, my family can't help me, the doctors can't help me, so I came to the revelation that only Jesus could help me. It was a hard reality but I was having trouble breathing. Life no longer was easy for me. I was struggling to bounce back and I wondered if I ever would. It wasn't just physical and mental but it was spiritual. I just did not understand. But, I was determined to get my life back; so, I kept pursuing God and searching the scriptures. There was a method to my madness. Some days were harder than others, but I was not going to give in to the enemy. I was going to fight with everything I had. Some days, it was a physical fight and on my weakest days it was a spiritual fight. As I continued on in my battle, I came across several key scriptures that help me through this difficult time in my life. Below, I will share a few of them as God reveals them for each situation.

FOR THE ATTACK ON MY BODY/LIFE: God revealed unto me a scripture from the Book of Job: *"Though he slay me, yet will I trust in him: but I will maintain mine own ways before him."* (Job 13:15 KJV) Let me tell you why I can trust Him after being slayed. Here, is a quick synopsis of my testimony. After four miscarriages, I found myself pregnant again. This time I was sure that I would bring this baby to term but this time not only did I lose the baby, but I almost lost my life. I ended up in hemorrhagic shock; simply meaning I bled to death. I was rushed to ICU as per protocol of the hospital, but yet life fading away. I arrived in ICU just in time to hear the doctors say she is not going to make it; all her blood is just about gone. As they continued to work on keeping me alive and putting IV's in and trying to stop the bleeding, I had my first experience and visitation from God. I remember His exact words to me even to this day. He said "Karen, your blood is gone; but mine is here. You shall live and not die and declare this, My Glory." Though, I had a long way to go this was the beginning of my intimate relationship with God. My trust was now truly in Him, because I had beaten the odds and lived without blood. I had become a walking and talking miracle. I was no longer walking in what I heard I was living proof of the Word.

FOR THE ATTACK ON MY MIND: God revealed to me two scriptures, one from the Book of Romans and the other from the Book of 2 Corinthians: *"And be not conformed to this world: but be* *ye transformed by the renewing of your mind, that ye may prove what is that good, and acceptable, and perfect, will of God"*- (Romans 12:2 (KJV). After coming out of ICU, the battle of the mind had begun. I still had the question of "Why?" As I begin to fight back, I needed something and someone to lead me in the way I should go. Even though, I was thankful for life I still couldn't understand the process. My mind had not transformed, even though my faith had increased. So, I continue to cry out to God for understanding and healing. He revealed to me many scriptures as He spoke to me in that still, small voice. Each time this happened, I was inspired, encouraged and healed little by little. I recognized my healing and understood it was going to take time. I got the revelation that I needed to go deeper because my scars ran deep. The deeper I went in the word, the stronger my relationship became with the Lord and the more knowledge and wisdom; I had begun to obtain. I had come to the realization that it was no longer just that one time experience or visitation with God, but it had now become a lifestyle. I was on my way to a breakthrough. No longer was I ignorant to the Word or the ways of God. For, my spiritual eyes had been opened and I could see and feel myself regaining life, health and strength. It was not an easy walk, nor was I completely healed; but I was learning how to live again.

And as I grew here came this next season, which gave me insight on how to work the word. *"Casting down imaginations, and every high thing that exalteth itself against the knowledge of God, and bringing into captivity every thought to the obedience of Christ;* (2 Corinthians 10:5-7 - KJV). Now, remember we are still dealing with the mind. Let me put it like this: whenever you go through hard times or bad situations people like to either blame you or use it against you. So, learning the word wasn't enough to keep you on solid ground. For the sake of your sanity, you had to learn to work the word. In other words, some people like to see you down and out and instead of helping you they try to hurt you. This is when you have to bring those words and thoughts into captivity and cast them down. For surely their words are not lining up with what Christ has said about you. You have to recognize that your Creator's Words are greater than the creations' words. However, we must also recognize that if our mind is not fed the proper thing your imagination can go wild. So, while you walking towards your healing it's imperative that you continue to prosper your soul; which are your emotions, intellect and imagination. Guard them with your life, because it truly can become the devils playground.

FOR THE ATTACK ON MY SPIRIT: God revealed to me a scripture from the Book of Romans: *"For I reckon that the sufferings of this present time are not worthy to be compared with the glory which shall be revealed in us"* (Romans 8:18 - KJV). Now, connected to your suffering comes a great attack on your spiritual life. It can either make you lose hope or increase your faith. The greater the attack on your body and mind the harder it becomes to have faith. Let me just be clear, when your faith in God is attacked your spiritual life gets weakened. However, I found out that the way God worked in me was He weakened the body to strengthen my faith. He continually showed me how the healing process is tied to my faith or belief. How words can heal you or kill you. That suffering is not a plot against your life but a plan to give you a new understanding on life. Suffering in my case took me to a new place in the spirit. For one, I learned to trust in a God I could not see. Second, I became a walking and talking miracle and last but not least; my faith was making me whole. For after all this suffering, I realized that at the end of this season; there was some glory that was so great that it totally outweighed and outshined my suffering. And that I would walk in a glory revealing stage and it would all be worth it. I had gotten to a place in my journey, where I no longer asked why; because I understood that it had all worked together for my good. I had been through the process and I was no longer bitter, but better. I was no longer hurt, but healed. I was no longer in a place where I could be tossed to and fro, but I could stand on sound doctrine of the Word. I, now walk in Gods power and anointing. My experience with God had changed my life forever. It was now time to walk in purpose; because my destiny was calling me. Now, I could truly say God had prepared me for the road ahead. His power and glory had been manifested in my life.

Now, that I have become full circle, here are some biblical principles to follow that restored me. Take heed for they are truly a pathway to this Christian walk. Not only did I use the principles God provided a great support system. Make no mistake a good support is a big key to your healing and restoration but use your discernment. My testimony and my life's experience is just a way of being transparent. It may not happen to you the same way it happened to me but the concepts work for us all. I truly wanted to make it clear that life is not always easy. For surely, if you trust God and follow His principles you will certainly live and breathe again; which brings me back to my original scripture, *"But he knoweth the way that l take: when he hath tried me, I shall come forth as gold"* (Job 23:10 - KJV). Though, you may not always know your way and plan in life nothing is surprising to God. He knows your way and He also knows the day you would recover. For truly your trying was just a test of your faith and now that you have come forth: **Welcome to your New Season. It's Time to Breathe Again!!!**

About The Author

Apostle Dr. Karen Deadwyler

Apostle Dr. Karen Deadwyler is the Visionary of Dr. Karen Deadwyler International, Willing Women of Worship Fellowship and the Executive Pastor of Glory Temple Ministries located in Baldwin, New York. She is married to her best friend Apostle Ronnie Deadwyler for 31 years and counting. Apostle Dr. Karen is an, Inspirational Empowerment Speaker, Preacher, Prophetess, Health Awareness Speaker (Nurse), Entrepreneur, Columnist and Author of three self-published books. Dr. Karen is a natural educator who teaches real life lessons with wisdom from the throne of God. She mentors both men and women in various aspects of their lives, mainly through healing and restoration. She is a "doer" of the word not only a hearer. She carefully teaches you how to apply the principles taught in the Word of God to your everyday life so that you may live in peace, prosperity, and love. For more info you can contact Apostle Dr. Karen Deadwyler on her website www.drkarendeadwylerintl.com

Chapter 2

One Last Breath

    God's unchanging plan for humanity is to have an intimate relationship and open fellowship with us. However, when sin entered into humanity through the act of disobedience, God could no longer dwell with him. A new covenant had to be established and the plan of redemption was implemented. Jesus was sent into the world to redeem us. As Jesus wrestled with this heavy task, he pleaded to the Father, if there is be any other way, remove this cup of suffering (Luke 22:42). There was no other way. He then submitted to the will of the Father to suffer for our sakes. "But he was pierced for our rebellion, crushed for our sins. He was beaten so we could be whole. He was whipped so we could be healed" (Isaiah 53:5 NLT). Our redemption is based upon Jesus' willingness to suffer in our place, to take on our shame, to be rejected by the Father, and to die. Mark 15:37 tells us that Jesus "cried with a loud voice, and breathed his last" (NKJV). With His last breath, our hope was restored!

In reflection of Christ's suffering, excruciating cry and last breath, the only relatable experience that comes to mind is the birthing of a child. With each pain more intense than the last, the mother is encouraged to breath. If at any instance she tenses up, she could potentially pass out. As she dilates, she experiences intensely sharp sensations. With each contraction, she pants in desperation and exhaustion to the point of almost giving up until that moment when the baby's head crowns. Overcome by the hours or days of labor and anguish the mother is encouraged to take one last breath and push. Often as her last breath is released it is accompanied with piercing screams. Once the child is pushed out, those screams transition into tears of overwhelming joy. Likewise, when Jesus took his last breath the veil of the temple was torn in two from top to bottom (Mark 15:38). The barrier [sin] which prevented us from walking with God was destroyed when the soldier pierced his side; blood and water gushed out (John 19:34). This release of fluids from his side symbolizes the birth of the church. Thus, the birthing of our redemption occurred as the result of Christ's death. To live as Christ, we are required to surrender our last breath.

Life is synonymous with breath. Furthermore, breathing is the evidence of life.

God holds in Him all life. "*The Spirit of God has made me, and the breath of the almighty gives me life*" (Job 33:4 KJV). In order to, walk into the promise of a redemptive new beginning; we must take one last breath. Throughout life, one will experience multiple instances in which, he or she must be willing to make a last effort; to take one last breath prior to stepping forth in faith. If we hold on to the failures of the past and hold our breath, ultimately, the promise on our life will fade away. We cannot afford to let prior pains and disappointments hinder us from pressing forth.

In reflection, I think back on when I had to make the decision to file for divorce; ending my first marriage. I fought many years to preserve the marriage. Often my efforts were in vain. There were so many times we were separated because of outside interference designed to keep us from unifying as husband and wife. As a result of the negative influences of others, I found myself spiraling into a pit of despair. I was plagued with low self-esteem, insecurities and a loss of purpose. I was overcome by a silent depression that I hid.

For years I held my breath. I only uttered to a few people of my struggles. I was silenced, unable to speak or cry out and unable to trust. I was suffocating and eventually all that God purposed in me would be lost. Unavailingly, I clung to my vows like someone trapped in the bottom of a well clings to a rope dangling aimlessly from above. I tugged hopelessly at that rope. Perhaps, one day someone above would pull me out. As I clung to that rope, I became entangled in a cord of falsehoods; which entwined me until I could no longer move. The rope wrapped itself around my every being, until I blacked out. If I continued to wrestle with this rope, I would have eventually hung myself. Divorce was never an option for me. I was fighting to give my children that two-parent home. I was fighting to overcome every stigma against my union to their father. I was wrestling against the whispers and plots of Satan to destroy us. I was holding my breath.

There came a time when we pursued counseling and were given specific instructions regarding relocation and a fresh start. My heart raced with every hope and possibility. Unfortunately, he was unable to cut the ropes which pulled at him. He left yet again. It was at that instant that the Lord spoke to my heart to release everything. I had to release in order to survive. If I hadn't my children would not have a mother. The torturous circumstances of mental anguish would destroy me.

Upon releasing (breathing), my physical and mental health improved instantaneously. The blemishes and darkness on my skin which afflicted me, faded. The extra weight I was carrying dropped off without dieting. I could think clearly. The fog gave way to light and depression lifted. In fact, I was actually battling with a virus prior to his leaving. Coincidentally, when he left that day, my sinus passages cleared. I was able to breath. The fever broke and the aches diminished. Surely, this was a sign that the oppression which was overtaking me was connected to the circumstance. In faith, I released everything and took that last breath. I allowed the past and every negative attachment to it to die. The veil over my life was then torn, and I could finally see the promise.

I can sense that many who read this will not like the fact that I am speaking on divorce. We have been partially taught regarding marriage and what it entails. As a result, many enter into the covenant in ignorance. God never meant for divorce to occur. It was permitted as a result of the hardness of men's hearts (Matthew 19:8). Oh trust me, I read through every scripture prior to making this decision. I would never tell anyone to divorce. For me however, it was necessary. Scripturally, I was vindicated.

As I look back, I stand in awe of the healing that has taken place in my life because I took one last breath. My children are able to have a healthy relationship with their father and me. Our families have blended seamlessly in a fashion that many on the outside cannot understand. I have been freed from the bondages of resentment, bitterness, hatred and unforgiveness. As the veil was torn in my life, I was able to take an unbiased and unrestricted view of those who invaded my marriage. I reached a point where I could release and say *"Father, forgive them for they know not what they do"* (Luke 23:24). I was able to protect my children from the wounds I suffered when my parents divorced because I didn't carry those negative feelings toward their father. Even in that, the curse that hovered over my childhood was broken. Every generational parental dysfunction was destroyed because now, I was healthy enough to teach my children to love; despite the imperfections of personality and circumstance. If I would have held onto that breath, I would not have experienced the beauty that God has unfolded before me.

As I mentioned, when Jesus cried out and released his last breath, the veil was torn. Following that, the soldier pierced his side. From the outpour of his blood and water the church was born. In my life, as the past died and the veil was torn, I too experienced a birth. The Lord was positioning me for ministry even during the years of brokenness. Now, through the healing of that brokenness, I was able to move forward. Furthermore, I was emptied and available for the overflow of His Spirit which equipped me to pour into others. In the same year of my divorce, I was ordained as an evangelist. The following year I married a man who is truly my best friend. Even in that, I had to release one last breath. I had to have faith that what happened before would not happen again. I had to believe differently concerning myself and God's purpose for my life. I had to silence the previous voices that caused me to question my value.

Being a divorced single mother of three boys was not exactly desirable by the standards of man. My prayers after my divorce were, "Lord, I am fine being by myself and I have no desire to date. But if you have someone for me, you must bring him to me. Let him be a man after your own heart, loving you first with all his heart. That way, I know he will love me the way he should. Lastly, let him be like my brother [I prayed this because I admired the man my younger brother had become]. That same night, I recall the Lord speaking to me after I put the children to bed. I was taking a nice hot bath complete with bubbles and candlelight as He spoke, "Who can find a virtuous woman? Your value has just increased" (Proverbs 31). In other words, my children and my experiences had not diminished my worth. Rather, God declared that I am now a ruby of extreme value. My price had just gone up! The cost to attain me as a wife had increased!

God answered all of my requests concerning a husband. The first conversation I ever had with him was mind-blowing. He messaged me scriptures that ministered to me in a time of difficulty even though I never told him what I was going through. His passion for the word of God is astonishing! We became fast friends. As an added bonus of proof, my husband even has the same birthdate as my brother. My husband and I have been blessed to travel the world ministering the gospel. In just a short time, God has blessed us to start a ministry and a business, purchase a home, purchase several newer cars, co-host on radio together, write books, minister internationally, have a child, and so much more. I can't even fathom what could have happened if I never took that one last breath to release the past, and allow it to die; if I never took that one last breath to allow my future to be birthed.

In the midst of personal crisis, customarily, we pray that the Lord intervene swiftly and bring relief. We have difficulty accepting suffering as our portion. We quote various scriptures in belief that we will soon experience restoration, redemption and vindication. However, the truth which most will not accept is that suffering is necessary. Pain is inevitable, and trials are unavoidable. In order to reign with Him we must suffer with Him (2 Timothy 2: 12). What's more is that we must die in Him in order to walk in the fullness of the redemption Christ has provided for us on the cross. Philippians 1:21 (KJV) tells us "For me to live is Christ, and to die is gain." Therefore, taking that one last breath is necessary to release our past so that our future can be birthed. Nevertheless, we must be mindful to release that breath because if we inhale and never exhale, that same oxygen cannot circulate. It will turn into poison inside our lungs eventually suffocating us. Breathing requires inhalation as well as exhalation. It is in the exhaling that release takes place. In order for promise to continue, some things must die. You must fully release that last breath.

My dear friends, I know that your life circumstances seem dreary. You have tried with all of your might to press through. You think by holding on, eventually the situation will turn around. However, I warn you that in holding on so tightly you are literally suffocating. I challenge you today to seek the Lord. Pray that He shows you the areas in your life where you need to release. As He reveals each to you one at a time, I challenge you to repent of the sins which accompany the failure to release. Repent of unforgiveness, unbelief, bitterness, strife, envy, jealousy, rage, murmuring, gossip, idolatry, covetousness, lying and even murder [by way of your words]. Now, with a loud cry; I command you to release. I command you take **ONE LAST BREATH!!! Let the past DIE!**

About The Author

Prophetess Renatta Parnell

Prophetess Renatta Parnell is a native of Pontiac, Michigan. At seven, she was baptized in Jesus' name and filled with the Holy Spirit. She is the wife to Pastor Jonathan Parnell and a mother of 5 children.

Renatta Parnell received much of her ministerial foundation through her father's ministry (Abiding Presence Ministries, Intl., – Apostle Gary Jones). In August 2009, she received her ministerial license from Pastor, Dr. Marie E. Brice (Pentecostal Church of Deliverance, Baltimore, MD). On July 1, 2012, Renatta Parnell was ordained evangelist by Apostle Trena D. Stephenson. In June of 2017, she was installed into the office of Prophet. She and her husband have been blessed to travel internationally with Bridge International Missions Alliance under the leadership of Apostle Trena D. Stephenson.

In March 2015, she and her husband Pastor Jonathan Parnell established Loved of God Ministries, International; a Biblical teaching ministry preparing the body of Christ to walk and operate in ministerial gifts for the furtherance of the Kingdom of God through outreach and evangelism.

Renatta Parnell currently holds a Master's of Science in Psychology from University of Phoenix. Her desire is to aid people in crisis by helping them to heal through their wounds. Through her business Just Blessed Enterprises, LLC. She serves as a Christian counselor, advocate, and mentor. She also volunteers in an organization which assists victims and survivors of human trafficking.

In addition, Renatta Parnell is also a published author and poet. She has written for JO Magazine, Dayton, OH and SOAR Magazine. She is also a contributing author for "And He Still Sees," "And He Still Waits," and "Seven Ingredients to and Effective Prayer Life Volume 7." Renatta Parnell has also co-hosted on "The Fullness of God" radio broadcast.

You may contact Prophetess Renatta Parnell for ministry via email at lovedofgodministries@gmail.com or for counseling at jblessedent@gmail.com.

Chapter 3

Finding Time to Pray

God spoke it so clearly and firmly in my heart to share these words given by Him to help others. Our prayer life is so important because, it lets the Father know how much we love Him and have His heart.

So, many of us have been petitioning God for what is happening in the world today; that they have missed the real purpose of praying for many other situations and problems that we are facing today. God states this, *"But when ye pray, use not vain repetitions, as the heathen do: for they think that they shall be heard for their much speaking"* (Matthew 6:7). God doesn't want us to keep repeatedly asking for prayers, as if He doesn't listen to us. He desires to give all good things to us, if we ask Him.

In prayer, as a Believer, you must prepare yourself to hear the Voice of the Father. The Father has not changed; we as Believers must make sure that we get into the water, meaning that we feed our spirit daily with God's pure Word daily. We must set aside a time for the Father and position ourselves in his presence. This shows the Father that meeting with Him in His Word has great value to you. Today, the Church has shown and taught many of us that if you repeatedly make your requests known you will get His attention.

God said, "it's time for you to stop spending all your time discussing media news, social network issues and even the many false promises, betrayal, rejections, disappointments, domestic violence, rape, etc., to name a few that have now become our daily life focus. God said that He's not far off somewhere; but His strategies and instructions have been given to us to take down those strongholds with Him in prayer." Fasting and praying will place the flesh under the order of Holy Spirit by hearing the voice of God's instructions of when, for what, and for whom you need to be praying will be revealed to you.

The Father says, "it's time for us to be on our knees, not to be on our knees when we are stressed and experiencing disappointments within our live or resorting to news media, gossiping and social network bashing. Prayer is a lifestyle that has been shared with us from the beginning of His Spoken Words. His instructions have always been to come with an open and committed heart before Him (the Father). Nehemiah 4:9, *"Nevertheless we made our prayer unto our God, and set a watch against them day and night, because of them."*

God will meet us when we set aside a time for fellowship, and he will speak to us. God is always looking for us for fellowship, He said, "He waits for us daily."

David prayed three times a day, look at Psalms 55:17 (ASV) *Evening, and morning, and at noonday, will I complain and moan; and he will hear my voice.* Daniel also prayed three times daily. It was also spoken by Jesus to His disciples to develop a consistent and persistent prayer life.

Jesus instructions to his disciples, Luke 11: 5-20 – *"And he said unto them, which of you shall have a friend, and shall go unto him at midnight, and say unto him, Friend, lend me three loaves; For a friend of mine in his journey is come to me, and I have nothing to set before him? And he from within shall answer and say. Trouble me not: the door is now shut, and my children are with me in bed: I cannot rise and* give thee. I say unto you, though he will rise and give him as many as he needeth. And I say unto you, Ask, and it shall be given you; seek, and ye shall find; knock, and it shall be opened unto you. For everyone that asketh receiveth; and he that seeketh findeth, and to him that knocketh it shall be opened." This kind of prayer comes by consistently praying until what we have is not only received but found and open to us.

Psalms 91: 1-7, "He that dwelleth in the secret place of the Highest shall abide under the shadow of the Almighty. I will say of the Lord; He is my refuge and my fortress: my God; in him will I trust. Evidently, he shall deliver thee from the snare of the fowler, and from the noisome pestilence He shall cover thee with his feathers, and under his wings shalt thou trust: his truth shall be thy shield and buckler. Thou shalt not be afraid for the terror by night; nor for the arrow that flieth by day; Nor for the pestilence that walketh in darkness; not for the destruction that wasteth at noonday. A thousand shall fall at thy side, and ten thousand at thy right hand; but shall not come nigh thee."

Let me share a time in my life that I had to get myself lined up with God's instructions, over a year ago my father became ill. I received a call from my sister, saying she rushed him to the hospital. Of course, I left from work traveling to be with him, asking God for favor to keep him until I got there. After speaking with the doctor, they informed my sister and I that he had Leukemia and at his age of 93 years old, his body wouldn't allow him to take the treatments.

Of course, being an intercessor and prayer warrior, I got before the Lord asking God to keep my Father; I needed him around and my mother passed over thirteen years ago. And really, I wasn't ready to be without him. He would always come and visit on holidays buying everyone gifts that he like and what he thought we needed. He was funny!

To fast forward, he was released under hospice care to us; since my older sister was his caretaker, we had to adjust their living arrangement. The hospice care agent only allowed us to move him to our daughter's house because she is a registered nurse and she would be able to provide the necessary care along with hospice caretaker, during his last days.

It was hard for me because we lived in a townhouse, he couldn't live with us. I was very hurt and I was still working every day. But my heart was with my Father. Each day, he was getting very uncomfortable, not sleeping and in pain daily. I decided that I would go and sit with him after work to pray and talk with him. It was hard some days; he knew it was me and other day's he thought I was someone from the hospice care facility visiting him. Many days he didn't recognize me at all or knew that I had been there to visit with him. Those days were very difficult for me, but I knew God had a plan for me too.

I would go home to pray at 7:00 pm every night, which was my special time to pray, asking God to heal my Father and bring comfort to my older sister and provide clarity on what was next for my Father. I don't ever remember waiting on God to provide his instructions about my concerns about his health. I thought that was what I suppose to do because he was my Dad.

One night my husband said, "Angie! You need to pick what days you are going to stay with your Dad; because you're now allowing your body to run down and you're not at all listening to God". He was right I just wanted to be with Him, because I felt I wasn't there for my Mother when she went home to be with the Father. I started thinking over what my husband had said and that night, God spoke to me and said, "You can keep doing it your way of handling this situation regarding your Father, but it's not my way". I really didn't understand what God meant that night, but it stayed heavy on my Spirit and each day I continued visiting my Dad.

The most impressive thing that God did for me was allowing me to be with Dad in the afternoon prior, but that following early morning; he asked me to just pray with Him. He wanted to make everything was right with the Father. After praying with him, he said, he would see me on Tuesday, evening after work. because he didn't want me any longer to come every day, he said rest. I never told him that I could skip a day, but God revealed it to my Dad. That was God's instruction to me the night before, not knowing that he was going to pass later that Sunday evening.

Our daughter shared with me, he got dressed up in his Sunday suit, after I left, waiting to go to church. He told our daughter that he was going to lay down on his bed, until she was ready to leave for church. She found him about half hour later with his hands on his lap. He was finally at peace, he passed and he went home to be with Lord. I got the call that afternoon, went to her house stayed with him until the hospice caretaker came to write-up the final paperwork. It was to me a long waiting period, but he was finally home.

We want to do all the right things when it comes to our loved ones, but God is all and all-knowing when it pertains to our love one's life purpose. If you need guidance stay in prayer with the Father, He will meet you there if you just wait on Him.

God is incredible, He never intended for us to experience pain. God places concerns and issues in perspective and provides answers to us; so, that we can have the right attitudes when dealing with pain and suffering. God never intended for us to experience any pains, God loves us. God sometimes allows pain for His Glory and purpose in our life. In John 11:4 – When Jesus heard that, He said: "This sickness is not unto death, but for the glory of God, that the Son of God might be glorified thereby."

God has set times and seasons during our life for us to come and fellowship with Him. He is looking for a set time from us.

Psalms 5: 1-3 says, *"Give ear to my words, O Lord consider my mediation. Hearken unto the voice of my cry, my King, and my God: for unto thee will I pray. My voice shalt thou hear in the morning, O Lord in the morning will I direct my prayer unto thee and will look up."*

Pray always without ceasing, pray for the purpose, for power, pray for release and please tarry and fast so you may receive his instructions.

We must be obedient to meet with the Father daily not once a day; but always, especially for our churches, nations, communities, families and regional areas. So, that we can honestly see and experience the Birth of God prayers.

We must set aside time to seek the Lord. "Seek the Lord, while He may be found, call upon Him while he is near" (Isaiah 55:6). God is waiting to instruct, guide and give us Wisdom and revelation to destroy the works of the enemy and to bring forth the Kingdom of God.

"Call unto me, and I will answer thee, and shew thee great and mighty things, which thou knowest not." (Jeremiah 33:3).

Prayer:

Father, I pray that any generational seed that has prevented and stopped us from planning and preparing us to hear from you at a set time during the day or night will go forth in Jesus Name. In the mighty Name of Jesus destroy the weapons of distraction and intimidations that the enemy uses to cause us to not walk in faith. I pray for divinity meets humanity. I pray for forgiveness and healing in the earth. Father I pray for spiritual growth and financial increase to the Body of Christ. I pray that God release Freedom to all that are bond. In Jesus Name, Amen.

About The Author

Apostle Angela Bradley

Angela Bradley is an Apostle, along with her loving husband Apostle Carnal, Founder and Overseer of The Plan Ministries and Life in the City Ministry.

Angela has a tremendous passion for God Word coupled with a love for God's people. She has a contagious spirit of generosity that flows through every faucet of her ministry. Pastor Angela often says, "I just want to do what God wants me to do and always be in the right position to hear His (God) voice." That's her motto. Her vision is uncompromisingly clear, with one central principle; to build and develop a Kingdom of empowered people for the Kingdom of God that they may establish a pure personal relationship with God.

She knows that praying always without ceasing and proclaiming the Word of God in every situation is what God is calling his people to do at this time. God has instructed and anointed her to continue to pray. So, that the movement and a repositioning takes place; for the work that is before us shall be accomplished. Whatever the Father says to her, you can guarantee she will do it without compromising or watering down God's Word.

Angela has been serving God's people for over forty-six years, but most remember as an awesome servant to God's people. She is an Author, a Real Women Certified Facilitator's and a Certified Mental Health First Aid for National Council for Behavioral Health.

She has two wonderful children Vincent and Tonoah; and six grandchildren and one great-granddaughter Mila, whom she loves dearly.

Chapter 4

The Secret to the Presence of God

"You awaken us to delight in your praise, for you made us for yourself, and our hearts are restless until they rest in you." The Confessions of Saint Augustine book 1 pg. 11. Who is the Holy Spirit? Can I really know Him? How do we enter into God's presence on a daily basis? How do I hear the voice of God? My objective in this writing is to really answer one question, "What is true prayer?" I believe that what I am going to share with you will change your life, and you will never be the same. My prayer for you is that as you read this chapter, you will rediscover if you have never known that from the very beginning God's desire is that we would live in His presence. I am certain that many questions you may have will be answered as we begin our journey into the presence of God.

My First Love

I was about five-years-old sitting on my Dad's lap in our home in Detroit, MI. We were watching a well-known and respected preacher on television. When I first saw him I asked, "Daddy, why does he have all those people in his service?" My Dad responded, "Son, it's because he was obedient to God." Even though, I didn't fully understand what I was seeing, I was amazed as this man of

God ministered to those who were sick. I was impressed by the demonstrations of the power of God. Each person would walk on the platform, and he would lay hands on them or blow. Then, they would fall to the floor. I recall how crowds of people would swarm the pulpit eagerly awaiting for him to pray for them.

As a child, I was curious to know what made them fall to the floor. I knew that I wanted to be like that someday so that I could help people. As a result, I would imitate what I saw on television. I would use my toys to set up my own little miracle service. Sometimes, I would also stand up on my stool imagining that I was in front of a large crowd of people ready to minister to the sick. I imitated the preacher, "Line up on my right and on my left, don't wait for me to call out your healing." On occasion, I would blow on my parents, siblings and relatives expecting them to fall to the floor. I remember going to preschool and kindergarten doing the same to my classmates. I got into trouble with my teacher who called my parents and said, "Your Son is spitting on people," not realizing, I was blowing on them. My parents didn't understand until they realized that I was imitating the preacher I saw on television. Of course, I didn't know any better at the time. Looking back, I realize that God was birthing something in me.

Today, I know with all of my heart that the Holy Spirit was giving me a glimpse of His purpose for my life. I did not know who the Holy Spirit was or that He was actually a person. In my spiritual hunger, I began to ask my father questions about God and the Bible. I didn't realize until years later, how hungry I was to know God; and that when I was born my parents dedicated me to the Lord. I remember when we relocated to our new home in Belleville, MI; the Holy Spirit began to touch my life in a very personal way. The Holy Spirit was the person drawing me to my bedroom to pray alone. He was a real person who I could not see, touch, or feel, but I knew that there was a precious presence with me. I felt as if I was developing a relationship with someone. Before this transpired in my life, I recalled the previous church my parents pastored. I remember going with my family every Sunday morning faithfully. We went to every Bible study, and every choir rehearsal. I heard the different Bible stories, and saw Bible movies. I always believed in God and what my parents told me about Him and Jesus. I remember being baptized and taking communion. Yet, something was missing.

It wasn't until we relocated, that I met and experienced the person of the Holy Spirit who began to touch my life and draw me to the Son of God. He made Jesus real to me. I gave my life to Jesus Christ at 12 years old and was saved. Afterwards, the hunger for Him exploded in my heart as the wisdom of God's word filled me while reading the scriptures in a new way. In reading the gospels my awareness heightened regarding the substance and reality of Jesus and the Holy Spirit. I knew that God was in heaven sitting on a throne, and Jesus was on His right hand. This experience was so real to me that I drew pictures of the rapture of the church, heaven and hell, and the second coming of Jesus to earth. During this time in my childhood, Jesus became increasingly real to me in such a dramatic way that I felt like he was in the same room with me. I developed a reverential fear for Him because I understood that He is HOLY. I was convicted of my sins and understood that His desire was for me to walk with Him and be cleansed by His blood on a daily basis.

The Holy Spirit is a real person. He is the Spirit of the Lord sent by Jesus to be with us always. Jesus said, *"It is expedient for you that I go away: for if I go not away, the Comforter will not come unto you; but if I depart, I will send him unto you. The Comforter, which is the Holy Spirit, whom the Father will send in my name, he shall teach you all things, and bring all things to your remembrance whatsoever I have said unto you"* (John 14:26-16:7). This same Holy Spirit, whom Jesus calls "The Comforter," said that He would abide with us forever. He is the one who would be called along our side to guide us into all truth. He reveals the revelation of Jesus Christ, and opens our eyes to the truth of the Bible. He manifests the work of the cross of Calvary, and He is the only one who can help us to pray and talk to God (Romans 8:26).

The Breath of the Holy Spirit

"Draw me, we will run after thee..." Song of Solomon 1:4. *"No man can come to me, except the Father which hath sent me draw him:"* John 6:44. *"Quicken us, and we will call upon thy name"* (Psalm 80:18). *"It is the spirit that quickeneth; the flesh profiteth nothing"*

(John 6:63). True prayer is waiting upon the Lord in silence until He quickens/moves you. Waiting upon the Lord in quietness causes the flesh to wither away and die, so that we can commune with Him and worship Him in spirit and in truth. Waiting upon the Lord alone is the key to getting into the spirit realm for ministry. It is what breaks up our fallow ground so that we can enter into God's presence and also experience the power of God as mentioned in Habakkuk 3:3 - 4.

Often times, when we read the scriptures and enter into prayer, we are unaware that when Jesus said, "ask, seek, and knock," He actually was giving us the roadmap into God's presence according to the pattern of the tabernacle of Moses. The tabernacle of Moses was divided into three sections. The first section is the outer court where the flesh surrenders to the Lord. The second section is the holy place where intimacy for Him is birthed because we surrender our soul. The third section is the holy of holies where our presence becomes His presence and we surrender our spirit. The holy of holies is where we become one in the spirit with Him. We cannot truly pray without waiting upon the Lord first, because He is holy and no flesh can dwell in His presence. Habakkuk 1:13 and Romans 3:20 tells us His eyes are too holy to look upon our sin. The Bible teaches us to let our words be few, by first making our petition known to Him and then being silent and still until He speaks and moves us to pray.

Isaiah 40:31 says, *"They that wait upon the Lord shall renew their strength; they shall mount up with wings as eagles; they shall run, and not be weary; and they shall walk, and not faint."* This passage of scripture gives us the secret to prayer. The eagle stands upon the rock patiently waiting for the right current, stretches out his wings, and soars while the wind takes him higher above the clouds and storms. Running means to catch up with the Master. As long as, we are behind the Master, we are at risk of neglecting fellowship with Him. Furthermore, we are no longer covered under His presence; thus, allowing an open door for the enemy. Waiting upon the Lord is not the absence of action; rather it is the motion of running back toward the cloud of His presence. Once we have returned to the safety of fellowship, we can then walk with Jesus. We redeem the time in the presence of Jesus. When we wait upon the Lord in stillness, it will cause the breath of the Holy Spirit to return to us. As a result, all of our spiritual senses are restored in His presence.

Another important reference is Psalm 40:1-2, *"I waited patiently for the Lord; and he inclined unto me, and heard my cry. He brought me up also out of a horrible pit, out of the miry clay, and set my feet upon a rock, and established my goings."* Waiting upon the Lord brings healing, deliverance, and success in every area of our lives. However, we must be willing to wait as long as it takes. The Bible says in Psalm 46:10, *"Be still and know that I am God."* The Hebrew word for still is "Raphah" meaning "to stay, draw, cease, forsake, and be alone." In Exodus 14:13, Moses told the children of Israel to *"stand still and see the salvation of the Lord."* Many of us today think we can come before the Lord with our hand out expecting for Him to meet our needs. We come before Him with a heart of selfishness, instead of a heart to serve and fellowship. It's time we realize that God has needs. His needs are most important. He longs for a face to face encounter with us behind the veil. He longs to spend time with us and to have an intimate powerful relationship with Him. If we really think we have waited a long time on Him, we should really ask the question of how long has God been waiting on man to get into the secret place with Him? How long has God been waiting for the restoration of relationship, we once had with Him in the beginning before the fall of man? If we truly want to know the Lord and His ways and if we want to receive His power then there is a price to pay. Undoubtedly, the price is high but it's worth the cost. The price requires our time and willingness to wait on Him. Our dedication to the word of God is also required. We must hunger and be willing to ask the Holy Spirit to reveal His truth. Ultimately, we must willingly submit our life. Of course, it is a choice because the Lord never forces His will on anyone. This is the secret to the presence of God.

Steps to invoke the presence of God

As you read this, I am sure you are wondering, "Jonathan, how do I practice this?" It's simple. First, set aside time for yourself. Secondly, find a private location for yourself. Third, you may want to change the atmosphere around you with soft worship music. Fourth, sit down or get on your knees. Be still and meditate on the Lord. It is also a great idea to read your Bible slowly and patiently. The more you practice this secret it will become easier and there will be a daily contact with the Master as you begin to carry His presence with you everywhere. A closer relationship will be birthed and you will begin to experience the strength of His peace as your soul is quieted. The chaos of the outside world will no longer move you. You will become like the deer of Psalm 42 who longed for the water brooks and jumped into the river of the presence of Jesus. As a result, the scent of the deer was lost to its prey. This is God's promise to us in Isaiah 30:15, which says in quietness and in confidence in Him shall be our strength. God also promises, "There is a path which no fowl knoweth, and which the vulture's eye hath not seen: The lion's whelps have not trodden it, nor the fierce lion passed by it" (Job 28:7-8). There is a place where Satan and his demons can no longer touch you or find you.

As I conclude, I want to encourage you to let this be your prayer every day,

"Dear Jesus: Let me pay the price, give me the heart that serves and waits upon you in silence and confidence because in your presence there is safety."

About The Author

Pastor Jonathan J.R.W Parnell

Jonathan J.R.W Parnell is the second of two children born to Pastors Rodney and Janet Parnell. He was born on August 25, 1987 in Detroit MI. Having accepted Jesus at an early age, he answered the call to the ministry in March 2007.

Jonathan is the husband of Prophetess Renatta Lynn Parnell and devoted father to their children. He is the founder and Pastor of Loved of God Ministries, International. Jonathan's passion is to take the gospel of the kingdom to the world, and to continue the original mandate of our Lord Jesus Christ. Jonathan and his wife have experienced the privilege of taking the gospel to Nigeria, Kenya, and South Africa. He has also authored in a previous Daughters of Distinction series, "7 Ingredients to an Effective Prayer Life," compiled by Trena D Stephenson.

As Jonathan continues his walk, he certainly will further his education both naturally and spiritually in "The Word of God," and fulfill the glorious commission of our Lord and Savior Jesus Christ.

Chapter 5

Gods Change Agents- Opening New Spiritual Doors

Be alert, be present. I'm about to do something brand new. It's bursting out! Don't you see it? There it is! I'm making a road through the desert, rivers in the badlands. There is a moment in time that can change your "Forever" — and prophetically, I declare to you ... it's on the way! Isaiah 43:19 (Message Bible)

In Isaiah 43:19 (English Standard Version), it reads: *"Behold, I am doing a new thing; now it springs forth, do you not perceive it? I will make a way in the wilderness and rivers in the desert."*

I want to emphasize to you today that, when you were bound by sin, God brought you forth out of darkness into His marvelous light. He is preparing you to be His Change Agent and He is Opening New Spiritual Doors for you. You were created to be a Change Agent by bringing others out of darkness into the light and revelation of Jesus Christ. "You are the light of the world" as promised in Matthew 5:14.

You are called to let your light shine before men so that they may see your Father's good work and glorify Him. God is the ultimate Change Agent. He is always making things new. God is the God of the present and He can turn your situation or circumstances around immediately. God doesn't need a 24-hour period because He is a right now God.

Elijah was able to turn a widow's life around in less than 23 hours. God told him to go to Zaraphet and that there would be a widow who would sustain the prophet of God while he was in town. She herself faced a hopeless situation because she was preparing her last meal for herself and her son due to the famine in the land. She said to the prophet, "I only have a little bit of meal and oil and after that, we are going to die". Elijah was able to be her Change Agent. On that day, Elijah said to her, "Make me a cake first." He was testing to see if she would put him and God first in her life- and if she did, she would be blessed. We know that she indeed believed in Elijah's request. The meal she prepared was a sacrifice and tested her faith, but in return from her obedience to the man of God, the oil lasted for many days and they ate daily and never lacked. God used Elijah as a Change Agent to turn this woman's circumstances around. Just imagine what He can do for you and anything you may be facing! God is looking for men and women to be Change Agents today in the earth realm to bring as many souls as possible into the Kingdom of God. We all have a part to play.

As I meditated on "God's Change Agents, Opening New Spiritual Doors", it reminded me how the Lord specifically designed and chose you and I to be His Change Agents here on earth. As we walk in our assignment, anointing, mission, and call given us at birth, we will be able to walk through any and all new spiritual doors that He opens for us in return. However, we must continue to stay in the word of God, pray, fast, praise, and worship the Lord as He continuously develops us to become His Change Agents.

To be a Change Agent for the Lord, the change must start with you first.

All change starts with us. The opening of new spiritual doors started the day you invited Jesus Christ into your life as your personal Lord and Savior. Jesus Christ said in John 14:12 (King James Version), *"Verily, verily, I say unto you, He that believeth on me, the works that I do shall he do also; and greater works than these shall he do; because I go unto my Father."*

Genesis 1:27-26 reminds us that the Lord said, *"Let Us make man in Our image, after Our likeness, to rule over the fish of the sea and the birds of the air, over the livestock, and over all the earth itself and every creature that crawls upon it."* So God created man in His own image; in the image of God He created him; male and female He created them. (Study Bible, KJV). The Lord has been using men and women for over 2,000 years as His Change Agents.

Agents such as Mary represent a touching example in the Bible of total surrender to the will of God.

Deborah, Israel's only female Judge was both a Prophetess and ruler of the people of ancient Israel. She was the only woman among the twelve Judges. Ruth was a virtuous young woman. She was so upright in character that her love story remains one of the most popular accounts in the entire Bible today.

Esther was also a Change Agent for the people of Israel. Her Uncle Mordecai uncovered a plot for destruction of the Israelite's by Haman, to have all her people killed. Esther, who was a Jew, became a Queen under the rule of King Xerxes of Persia. You can read about that in Esther Chapter 2. Mordecai, her Uncle enlisted the help of Esther. Esther is one of only two books in the Bible that is named after a woman.

Let's look at Esther 4:13-14, it says, *"Mordecai sent this reply to Esther: "Don't think for a moment that because you're in the palace you will escape when all other Jews are killed. If you keep quiet at a time like this, deliverance and relief for the Jews will arise from some other place, but you and your relatives will die. Who knows if perhaps you were made a king and queen for just such a time as this?"* This is a powerful reminder of how God will call those whom He wants to use as His Change Agents.

There were several men in the Bible that I believe were God's Changes Agents, role models and who also demonstrated major influence in the history of the Bible. For example, Moses was a godly man that struggled with failure, but that didn't hinder or stop Moses. He became a man consistently in tune with the Lord's plan. He loved the people of Israel who God called him lead. Moses was a man who repented without hesitation when he disappointed the Lord. His accomplishments astonished him as one of God's Change Agents.

Joshua rose to recognition as Moses led Israel out of Egypt. He was selected as one of the spies to enter the land that God promised Israel. Many of the spies returned with a discouraging report of the land God had promised Israel, but Joshua and Caleb reported all the wonderful things that God could provide in Canaan. Joshua trusted God and his patience was unusual. Joshua was known as a strong leader of Israel.

David was well-known in the Bible as a man who followed God and was sensitive to the leadership of God in his life. David was a man after God's heart. He didn't have a problem repenting. Many of the Psalms in the Bible were written by David. He never allowed his circumstances, trials or tribulations to discourage him or get him off-focus. All of these men were used as God's Change Agents. Look at the history, innovation, and impact they made on the lives of others without anyone's assistance aside from the Holy Spirit.

Noah was known for being righteous and the prominent ark he built to survive the severe storm. He branded himself as a survivor who made sure his family and many animals were saved. Noah wasn't selfish or disobedient. He set the standards of team work, unity and innovation that marked his as a Change Agent who made a difference for everyone to know how to survive while walking in God's wisdom and discernment. Noah set the standards that all Change Agents can follow by yielding and obedience.

Jesus selected Peter as one of his closest friends who demonstrated the "Characteristics of a Change Agent". Peter was faithful, focused, and committed. Even though Peter denied Jesus Christ three times, he still used Peter to spread the Gospel and allowed His light to sign through Peter. What an example of how even in failing the Lord, He still will use you to bring Him honor and glory as one of his Change Agents.

God is no respecter of persons. The same way He used these ordinary men and women as Change Agents that brought Him honor and glory, He can use you and I. However, we must surrender, yield and walk in obedience to Him and the call He has on our lives as His Change Agents. We must always go before the Lord for instructions. In being one of God's Change Agents, we should remember that change starts with us first.

"Jesus Christ is the same yesterday and today and forever" (Hebrew 13:8, KJV). "Every good and perfect gift is from above, coming down from the Father of the heavenly lights, who does not change like shifting shadows" (James 1:17, KJV). These two scriptures let us know that only one person is the same always; that is Jesus Christ in the Word of God. Anything we have or do is only because of Jesus Christ.

Change Agents are designed by the Lord to make a difference in the entire world wherever we go. The Lord said in Matthew 5:13-14. *"You are the salt of the earth. But if the salt loses its savor, how can it be made salty again? It is no longer good for anything, except to be thrown out and trampled by men." "You are the light of the world. A city on a hill cannot be hidden."* As God's Change Agents, begin to walk as a representative of the Lord and allow His influence, power and anointing to surround you, your gifts and talents as he uses you to change the world for the better. Change Agents are problem solvers. The Lord created us to solve problems, make the world a better place and bring him honor and glory. Many people are seeking visionary people who can provide solutions to the problems they face Change

Agents training manual is the Bible, the Holy Spirit, prayer, fasting and seeking wisdom and discernment from the Lord.

Every Change Agent or Christian has the potential to cause a negative or positive change in the entire world. However, as a child of the highest God, our responsibility is to cause positive change only. In operating as God's Change Agent, we have the power from the Lord to impact change of behavior, attitude and atmosphere because of the anointing that's on our lives. We can improve or impact the values of the secular, what others believe as important, how things are done and what can be condemned as long as we walk in the authority that the Lord's Word says we have in him.

All the Change Agents in the Bible promoted and enabled change to happen within any group, organization, business, the Body of Christ, Kingdom of God and wherever Jesus sent them. We can be the same type of Change Agent. Every Change Agent has the same characteristics. They:

- Possess unblemished vision
- Can endure long-suffering yet remain persistent
- Ask hard-hitting questions
- Are knowledgeable and lead by example
- Create strong relationships built on trust and integrity.

You and I have been chosen by the Lord to be His Change Agents to Open New Spiritual Doors and bring the good news of the Gospel to those that need it. Seek the Lord for His wisdom, discernment, revelation and knowledge as you carry out the responsibility of His Change Agents. In my years of being one of God's Change Agents, I have received a revelation that I am not assigned to everyone. In fact, I now understand the Lord's discernment and wisdom in following His guidance about who I am assigned to.

<u>Some Spiritual Vitamins for God's Change Agent</u>:

> ➤ Study and meditate on the Word of God

- Know the voice of God
- Seek Godly counsel if you need guidance
- Make the Holy Spirit your Best Friend
- Operate in integrity and be a woman or man of your word
- Line up your words with your actions
- Seek God for wisdom and discernment daily
- Pray for God's guidance & direction before committing
- Self-Love is very important – have a TLC Day for you regularly
- Exercise must be a part of your life
- Put your total trust in God and depend on Him

God said in Jeremiah 29:11, "For I know the plans I have for you," declares the LORD, "plans to prosper you and not to harm you, plans to give you hope and a future."

Prayer:

Lord, thank you for allowing all of us to be a Change Agent just like you. And for Opening Spiritual Doors as we move forward in the journey you have planned for us.

God Bless You All – God's Change Agents

About The Author

Jacqueline "Jackie" Anderson

Ms. Anderson, a native of Baltimore and graduate of Coppin State, is the daughter of Edward Anderson and Beatrice Ward. Currently, under the covering of Apostle Patricia A. Stewart, Founder of International Prayer of Faith Ministries (IPFM). She has had the honor of serving in a variety of capacities in the Body of Christ: while under Bishop Bertha Greene, she Lead and Liaison Sacred Zion Full Gospel Church Prison Ministry, served as a Trustee, and a member of the Intercessory Ministry. At Zamar Worship Center & Ministries, Inc., she served as the Marketing/Resource Liaison. Pastor Samuel & Geraldine Burns from Bread of Life Full Gospel are Jackie's Spiritual Parents in the Lord. Jackie's faith is deeply rooted in the Word of God and His promises. Jackie designed a Gospel Salvation Track in 2014, to spread the gospel internationally and worldwide. She shares her spiritual love with everyone she meets!

Ministry & Personal Highlights:
- Bachelor of Science in Management Science
- Personal Assistant/ Marketing Liaison/Resource Specialist and Nursing Home Volunteer (IPFM)for Apostle Patricia A. Stewart, (IPFM)
- Networker and problem-solver
- Mentor and instructor with Youth Writer's Rock Nonprofit organization, Baltimore, MD
- Teen mentor and Volunteer of the Young Educated Sisters and Studio A, Baltimore, MD
- Volunteer & Advocate for Maryland Center for Veterans Education and Training in honor

- of her brother Ronald M. Jackson
- Passionate about empowering, encouraging, and networking with others to equip saints to reach their destiny and fulfill their purpose in the Kingdom of God

Quote to Live By:
I am walking in greater. "My gifts & talents make room for me, my gifts & talents will bring me before great men" (Proverbs 18:16).

Contact:

Email: jcdarius@aol.com
Cell: 410-736-1166

Chapter 6

Come Up Out of the Ashes

I had become bound (like a captive/prisoner) by the things that had occurred in my life through the actions of people being used by the enemy. God told me one day as I had encountered another situation to cause me to be hurt (my feelings became hurt by what was said to me) and I retreated that day to isolation again. I just laid in my bed and pondered on what happened that day and I started to allow it to consume my thoughts and it started to take me deeper into a depressed mode. Please know the enemy wanted me to become depressed and frustrated he wanted me to remain feeling hurt and to keep me from moving forward in my calling for God's purpose for my life. The enemy is not concerned about you if you are not doing anything to effect his kingdom here on earth. We are called to bring the gospel to the lives of people to be changed and transformed through the message of Jesus Christ.

In Ephesians 6:12, it states: *"For we wrestle not against flesh and blood, but against principalities, against powers, against the rulers of the darkness of this world, against spiritual wickedness in high places."* If the enemy could use the people dearest to me to cause hurt and pain and keep me isolated from fellowship with God and other Christians. This would keep me from rising up and standing as the warrior I know that I am. This is just what the enemy wants, to keep us down and keeping our mouths shut from praying and proclaiming the word of God over our lives, families, and others. If He (Satan) is trying to keep your mouth shut, this should pose a question; "Is the enemy threated when I open my mouth to pray?" Look back over your life, "What impact has God used you for His Kingdom?" This is not to glorify self but to glorify what God has done through you as His instrument. Has it caused a threat to his (Satan's) kingdom here on earth? If so, why wouldn't he target you?

Now, back to when I retreated and laid in my bed. I laid there allowing so many things to consume my mind, instead of focusing on God. Isaiah 26:3,"*You will keep in perfect peace all who trust in you, all whose thoughts are fixed on you!*" I wasn't focused on His word, only the situations I had encountered. When we allow our mind to be consumed with things that hurt us, it consumes us; we allow it to become illuminated, instead of allowing the word of God to be illuminated over the situation. This reminds me of the story of Peter walking on the water to Jesus (Matthew 14:22-23) and he started out focused on Jesus, but as he heard the boisterous waves from the sea; he took his focus off Jesus and started to sink.

However, the day I heard the Lord say, "Come Up Out of the Ashes", then I looked around the room like I was hearing things. Then I said, "what Lord", He said it again, "Come Up Out of the Ashes." I said, "Come Up Out of the Ashes. What does that mean Lord?" I began to google to find the word "ashes" in scripture and I came across Isaiah 61:3 (KJV) – "*To appoint unto them that mourn in Zion, to give unto them beauty for ashes, the oil of joy for mourning, the garment of praise for the spirit of heaviness; that they might be called trees of righteousness, the planting of the LORD, that he might be glorified.*" I heard the Lord say your ashes held you captive.

People can get confused or just don't want to understand what their call is by God. They feel they may lose your friendship, 'kicking it' the way you used to but when you are in Christ you are a new creature. Something certainly has to change to show you have been impacted by the Gospel of Christ. We were not called into the Kingdom to stay the same way we were before we received Jesus Christ as our Savior. A new creature becomes a part of God environment once they know they're no longer a sinner but saved by His grace.

I encountered several ashes that I had to come up out of, see as you continue to read. I was allowing them (ashes) to cover – bury me like a heap of wet leaves. We all know that when leaves get wet, they become very heavy to lift. The ashes weighed me way down and it truly was hard in my own strength to get back up again. The spirit of heaviness was certainly upon me deeply. Only for God who said as a reminder to me according to Hebrews 13:5-6 NLT"… *For God has said, "I will never fail you. I will never abandon you." So we can say with confidence, "The LORD is my helper, so I will have no fear. What can mere people do to me?"*

I was looking to others to help me out of this spiritual nightmare (spiritual warfare) but all they could do is pray for me.

Do you know the story about the lame man who was lying at the pool of Bethesda? He was waiting on someone to help him in the pool but when Jesus saw him according to John 5:6-9 *"When Jesus saw him and knew he had been ill for a long time, he asked him, "Would you like to get well?" I can't, sir," the sick man said, for I have no one to put me into the pool when the water bubbles up. Someone else always gets there ahead of me. Jesus told him, "Stand up, pick up your mat, and walk!" Instantly, the man was healed! He rolled up his sleeping mat and began walking!…"*

I had become in a sense like this lame man. Let's define word "Lame" according to the online KJV Dictionary it means - crippled or disabled in a limb, or otherwise injured so as to be unsound and impaired in strength; as a lame arm or leg, or a person lame in one leg.

So, truly this definition covers how I felt and what I was going through. I was spiritually lame and was not walking by faith, but what I felt because of my ashes. I felt like I can't walk by faith because I had lost my confidence and was lacking in faith. However, I had to take up my bed and walk – because truly God had already healed me from what I had experienced, but sometimes we can keep replaying in our minds our ashes – like watching the same movie over and over again until it keeps us stuck and covered in them even more. But by taking up my bed and walking according to 2 Corinthians 5:7 KJV, *"For we walk by faith, not by sight:"* I took up my bed which is to represent my faith, but at first I was laying down on my faith (bed) and not walking by faith. When I lifted my bed (faith) it lifted me up out of my ashes. I was already healed but I had to apply my faith according to Hebrews 11:1 Now faith is the substance of things hoped for, the evidence of things not seen. Sometimes, we are looking to see the change in our environment, before walking it out by faith; because, we serve a God that move on our behalf when faith is applied.

    Mind you, I had been going through allowing these ashes to cover and control– bury me for nearly a year. I had allowed more situations that kept occurring and piling on top of me instead of allowing God to bury my ashes. I was getting attacked on every side the enemy was using words spoken by others to try to condemn me or make me feel condemned. The enemy was telling who I was not in Christ and what I believed was wrong. But the bible tells us as believers in Jesus Christ in 2 Corinthians 4:8-9 (NLT),

"We are pressed on every side by troubles, but we are not crushed. We are perplexed, but not driven to despair. We are hunted down, but never abandoned by God. We get knocked down, but we are not destroyed."

And in Romans 8:34-38 (NLT), "Who then will condemn us? No one—for Christ Jesus died for us and was raised to life for us, and he is sitting in the place of honor at God's right hand, pleading for us. Can anything ever separate us from Christ's love?" Does it mean he no longer loves us if we have trouble or calamity, or are persecuted, or hungry, or destitute, or in danger, or threatened with death? As the Scriptures say, "For your sake we are killed every day; we are being slaughtered like sheep." No, despite all these things, overwhelming victory is ours through Christ, who loved us. And I am convinced that nothing can ever separate us from God's love. Neither death nor life, neither angels nor demons, neither our fears for today nor our worries about tomorrow—not even the powers of hell can separate us from God's love." God will never allow the enemy to overtake you when you are His. He will only allow but so much, He will never allow you to drift so far when you are His.

Remember, His sheep hears His voice according to John 10:27 (KJV), *"My sheep hear my voice, and I know them, and they follow me:"* I was hearing the Lord; I keep trying at times to respond by trying to get back up again.

Once again, the ashes were holding me captive like the Israelites suffered captivity for their wrong doing – sinning against God and they were overtaken by their enemies until they cried and reached out to God and surrendered and received deliverance. Do we allow the ashes to overtake you? The ashes don't mean we have sinned; however, we allow it to have power over us. Or do we instead look to the Almighty One that has all power in His hands.

Do we unknowingly make people our God? Exodus 20:3 (NLT), "You must not have any other god but me." We can replace God with people in our lives as god and not even realize we have done it. Basically, we placed them on the throne seat of our hearts. My consistent prayer has always been according to Psalm 139:23-24 (NLT), "Search me, O God, and know my heart; test me and know my anxious thoughts. Point out anything in me that offends you, and lead me along the path of everlasting life." Thank God, He reveals these things to us; so, that we can repent and get back on track with Him. He is so loving and merciful.

Now, let me share more of the ashes:

Betrayal, hurt, pain, disappointment, grief, shame, and feeling like a failure. I can share these things, why, because I'm free and no longer bound/captive to my ashes.

The Bible tells us in Matthew 5:44-45 (NLT), "But I say, love your enemies! Pray for those who persecute you!" In that way, you will be acting as true children of your Father in heaven… and according to Matthew 6:14-15 (NLT), "If you forgive those who sin against you, your heavenly Father will forgive you. But if you refuse to forgive others, your Father will not forgive your sins."

I don't look like what I have been through, and I'm no longer covered in ashes, but I know I have been given the 'beauty of ashes' – the oil of joy for mourning, the garment of praise for the spirit of heaviness; and I want encourage you to remember the same power that raised Jesus Christ from the dead lives on the inside of believers (You), and as a sister-in-Christ once said, "If you have the resurrecting power of Jesus Christ living on the inside of you, then you have the power to rise up out of every dead work that is trying to kill you. Rise up today and live." But I will put it this way; Arise and come up out of the ashes and live ~ Breathe Again!

About The Author

Pastor Tammy McNair

Pastor Tammy McNair is a compassionate and gifted preacher of the Gospel of Jesus Christ, she has a heart to serve God's people with humility, pureness, integrity, and to encourage and empower them in the Lord. She is the founder of Sister Circle Ministries in Waldorf, Maryland. She is married to Keith McNair, Sr. of 26 years and have three beautiful gifts from God: Vaneese (Kyle), Keith Jr., and Joseph and two granddaughters Kyeira Lorraine and Vanna Lee. She stands in faith according to Matthew 19:26...with God all things are possible.

To read more of her bio, log onto w ww.SCMinistries04.com.

Chapter 7

I am Persuaded - Persuaded I Am

There are always life examples and teachable moments. I have lived out some, quoted some and even kept some to myself. Some of these examples and teachable moments I will share and give their significance and meaning. It is very unique how Apostle Paul—being a murderer and arresting officer to the believers of Christ—was converted and became a witness who testified the very opposite of the belief he once had. The scripture brings out the fact that he had to prove himself to be a Christian because of his prior life's choices and decisions. Well, I praise God that I am able to say that I have endured the trials and pitfalls of life because of some of my life choices. And with every trial, I stand to bear witness that it is proven to me that there is a God; being the author and the finisher of my faith and not just a higher being, as some will say. I have not had the best life; there is always a story to tell, sometimes the story is worse than "the one before." But as the 'saints of old' would say "You can't tell it; let me tell it!" I am who I am today; because of what the Lord has done for me and that is just right for me! I am persuaded; persuaded I am!

The overall importance of being connected with God and living a life that is pleasing to Him is knowing that your life has changed for the better. I already know it might seem hard, because it can be very hard at times. We must remain focused on the fact that God will never leave us nor forsake us; He will lead us, guide us and bless us. In addition to, earthly gain; there is a reward in Glory that we can look for. Be mindful that living a life that is pleasing to God does not always mean there will be no issue or failure, as some may think. There have been many failures in my life. I am bold enough to admit that I was the cause of some of those. But when I think of the goodness of God and all that He has done for me—having His Jehovah Shalom, His Jehovah Jireh, His Jehovah Rapha (I could go on and on)—I can do nothing but praise Him. "If I had ten thousand tongues," as my grandmother would say, I could not tell it all (and I can talk)! I am persuaded; persuaded I am!

In my early life as a child, I remember leaning on God as a young boy. There were times when our family did not have a lot. He provided water from a spring. We had to get the water with old used milk jugs from other people's houses. We would even go to our neighbors' houses to borrow their jugs—knowing that we were not even welcomed. But God provided. There were times when our meals consisted of syrup sandwiches and cold cheese sandwiches. We had use of an outhouse in the middle field; brown paper bags would be used for toilet paper when we could spare none. As a boy, I did foolish things. I used to walk on the river when it was frozen, hear the cracking noises in the middle, and then try to run to other side—hearing later that some have drowned in the water doing the very same thing. I was not lucky; I was blessed. On that very same river, I would walk in low tide to find clams and would get stuck in the mud with nobody to help you! When I look back, I had my Jehovah Immeka—The Lord is with you. There were times then (and now) when I felt like I was in a pit and had to remind myself that He did not and would not bring me this far to leave me. Even today, I know I am a child of the most high God and trust him in every way. I do not focus on the situation; I put my focus on the word "victory." I am persuaded; persuaded I am!

My vision is that I see better ahead of me. The process and the "getting there" might look messy and not make any sense but I am reminded of the scripture in Romans 8:31 that states, "… If God be for us, who can be against us?" If He is on our side, then the whole entire world can not match up. What do we say to these things? Issues, problems, and the headaches associated with the crazy moments when you feel like giving up. We stand flat-footed and say, *"If God be for us, who can be against us?"* I know some will say that this is an excuse or cop-out; in some cases, they may be right. But it was not easy to be taken, beaten, whipped, pierced, and aware of the fact that He came to die, but Jesus knew that His Father in Heaven was for Him. He still asked if it was possible to let "this cup pass." Jesus saw and knew what was ahead. In spite of, all He endured; He knew that His better was ahead of him. The problem with many people is that they do not recognize God's might. So, they have no explanation at all. They have no excuse at all; for them, a good excuse is no excuse. It is time to stop making excuses and see that there was and still is a plan for all of us. I am persuaded; persuaded I am!

In present day, I see children hooked on drugs; they do not see that plan for their own lives. I am taken back to the times when there were Friday night "grow parties" and I found the "dusting" on the mirror that was left in the bathroom, because we, the children, had to stay in the bedroom. I am taken back to the times when I found the beer cans that were left with residue particles on the top with pen holes and black smoke on the can. All of that could have been me now. But, God had a plan for me; I had my Jehovah Mephalti – The Lord is a Deliverer. I thank God that He had better in store for me. There were some that would say they wanted better but would not let the mess they were involved with go. Romans 8:39 tells us that "Nor height, nor depth nor any other creature, shall be able to separate us from the love of God, which is in Christ Jesus our Lord." I could have given up, but He been too good to me. I would not have separated myself from God's love and missed being a part of the great plan He laid out for my ministry and my life. Even in my foolishness, He still made ways. God has always been faithful. And knowing this, I am stronger in Him. Thank God for people pouring into my life—looking past all of my issues and helping me because they saw purpose and destiny in my life. I am persuaded; persuaded I am!

I am the encore and not the decor. Now, I am preaching and teaching, truly, under the anointing that does not just break the yoke, but destroys it. We need to encourage others instead by loving them and telling them the truth. I am persuaded; persuaded I am that He loves me and know that He loves you too. Trust in Him; do not look at man, but look to God. I came to understand that even when there are things that happen that are not in my favor, God has a divine plan, and my life is in his hand. After all is said and done, I can truly live in Romans 8:1 -- I can and really say Romans 8:1, which says, "There is therefore now no condemnation to them which are in Christ Jesus, who walk not after the flesh, but after the Spirit." I am persuaded; persuaded I am!

About The Author

Chief Apostle Antonio Donald

Chief Apostle Antonio Donald was born November 5, 1978 to Howard and Virginia Donald, but was raised by his grandmother Mattie Snow Donald. He is a devoted Pastor, husband, and father. Living in expectation of the promise of the Lord, God has anointed him in many different areas of ministry. Ephesians teaches us that the true spiritual leaders use their gifts to equip God's people to do the work that they have been called to do; therefore, Apostle Donald has many sons and daughters in the ministry. He walks in the totality of the scripture set out in Isaiah 61; he recognizes and honors the Favor of the Lord that is on his life.

In terms of ministry work, Apostle Donald:

- Served as the Jr. Bishop and Overseer of The Spirit of The House of Worship in Chesapeake, Virginia;
- One of the founders of Tabernacle of Faith Church of Hayes, Virginia;
- Began a new ministry named "The Church" True Word Apostolic Ministries—leaving the Apostolic Church of Christ, Incorporated;
- Served as the Apostle of three churches in Jamaica, West Indies. (Bethel Town, Knioval and Bynside);
- Chief Consecrator, and affirmed Apostle, Prophet, Evangelist, Consecrated Pastor, and Anointed Teacher;
- Overall, has 28 plus years in ministry.

Apostle Donald is a graduate of James Dussault University's International Overcoming College of Religion, which is accredited by the World Wide Accreditation Commission (WWAC). He has an earned BBA in Theology, MA in Theology with a concentration in pastoral counseling, and Ph.D. in Theology.

Apostle Donald is married to Pastor Sytauri Q. Donald. Together, they have two BEAUTIFUL children: a son Eliel and a daughter Jahdai.

Chapter 8

Stolen Breaths

I remember it like it was yesterday. In my mind, there wasn't anything remotely different or significantly intriguing about that day than any other. While relaxing and lying calmly in my bed around 10:00 p.m. that night, I suddenly remembered the day prior having an interesting conversation with a unique gentleman. He made me promise to read a particular chapter in the Book of Revelation. So, I took that time to uphold my promise.

As I read the second half of the scripture, my eyes got extremely heavy. The more I read the heavier my eyes became, and it wasn't because I was sleepy. "Wake up Samantha!" perhaps me sitting up would work I thought, however, my eyes dropped even lower. As soon as, I read the last word my eyes shut. Something shut them and it wasn't me. Consciously, I heard a knock three times at the bedroom door. My eyes open and I saw a tall dark figure at the threshold of the door wearing a black trench coat with a tall black top hat. The dark figure pinned me to the bed. "I can't move." Paralyzed with fear; I tried calling Cassy, my then girlfriend, and not one sound came from my lips. Now, I'm freaking out! I could say her name in my mind, but I couldn't verbalize it. I had a crazy notion to say Jesus. I didn't think about it I just did it. As I called His name, "JESUS!" whatever that was going on immediately stopped. My body sat up seemingly on its own. And as soon as, I sat up it happened again. It slammed and pinned me back onto the bed. And again, I called on Cassy and again nothing happened. I figured since Jesus worked the first time it will work the second time. "JESUS!" I called. Nothing happened. Now, I'm truly losing it! My lips won't even move. By this time, it's even hard to think on the name Jesus, but I said it again in my mind. I noticed the more I thought on the name of Jesus the easier it was to move. JESUS! JESUS! JESUS! I kept repeating over and over in my mind until the name of Jesus began to formulate on my lips. "JESUS!!", I said loudly. Again, my body sat up. I had full activity of my limbs, but I was panting profusely and out of breath, like someone knocked the wind out of me. In a matter of seconds, it happened again! It was stronger than the time before. I figured there was really no need to call on Cassy. Her name had been a waste of time. So, I called on Jesus. It felt like I was in the fight of my life. I'm so confused. I have no idea what's going on. Yet, I continue to call his name. My body is so tired, I feel completely drained but I continued to call on His name because it just simply felt right. It was like something within me that just wouldn't let me give up. I screamed "JESUS!" I sat up in the bed closed the bible, ran into the living room franticly and told Cassy what happened; she proceeds to laugh at me. At this point, I don't know what to think. I do know one thing I don't want this bible nowhere near me. I walked swiftly to the dumpster, prayed over the bible and asked God to forgive me; if I'm wrong for tossing it, then I chucked it! All I recall is how the attack affected my breathing.

As I now reflect back, I realized the devil has been attacking my life; because he has been losing his authority upon me giving my life to Christ. Thirty-five years credited to him for rejection of never knowing my earthy father, the pain of abandonment and feeling unprotected by my mother, scared by abusive relationships and very deep soul wounds incurred by a life a promiscuity. I am still allowing the Lord to unravel the fragile places in me. He is restoring me piece by piece. Even though, I questioned God's presence in it all and had constant monologues with Him of my disdain for His lack of being in my life in all this chaos. I really wanted to know (like any sane person), why my life seemed so messed up compared to others. I needed to know what most people ask themselves. Why am I here? What is my purpose? Why me? I wrestled in prayer for a long time with these brutal conversations with God. The truth is the enemy didn't want me to breathe again. He desired to destroy my purpose. See, the parallelism in it all. He attempted to muzzle me and restrict me from the truth. Ultimately, in the end; I saw the truth. This experience changed my perspective from God's hatred of me to His love trying to save me from the dysfunctional and truly demonic childhood. This created an urgency to solidify my stance as a true believer and build a true hatred for the enemy's attempt to take my breath away. In this moment, I recognized the devil did not want me to breathe again.

One of the greatest lessons, I have learned in my life is how to catch my breath. I can only imagine how the birth experience is for newborn babies; when they take their first breath in this cold world, unknowing, of what the future holds. Although, a newborn is clueless about life; he or she accepts the gift of breathing and begins to live its life. I've learned that breathing goes beyond inhaling and exhaling, which is necessary for the body to receive oxygen to the blood; therefore keeping the body alive. As it is in the natural; so, it is in the spirit. We need the breath of the Holy Spirit to help us function in this thing called life. I can't help, but to be taken back to the creation account in Genesis; where God's own breath becomes Adam's breath and thus, also, our own. Breath is something we have all taken for granted, of course, until we can't or it becomes difficult. Giving the ability to breathe again is powerful, because; it is an indicator that no matter what has transpired in our lives, we can ask the Father to breathe new life within us. Job 33:4 (ESV), *'The Spirit of God has made me, and the breath of the almighty gives me life.'* We all need room to breathe.

Breathing again is powerful because it reminds us that no matter what has transpired in our lives, we can find ways to grasp that breath that reminds you that you are alive. Right here and now! You are alive, so it is time breathe again. It is time to learn how to breathe again. It is time to gain the needed tools for this season of your life; so that, the Father can remove limitations that are laying themselves upon you as you attempt to move. When Jesus requested the lame to take up their bed and walk, He did not ask them if they have the strength to do so. When He spoke the words, the power of the words in the Word (John 1:1) gave healing and strength to the body. Therefore, I speak to those of you who are tired of fighting and have been experiencing seasons of lack, repetitious patterns, cycles and loss of direction. May I encourage you to know that you can breathe again too. Psalms 61:3 (MSG) – "You've always given me breathing room, a place to get away from it all…" Know that you can breathe again, too. This time you won't just fight to protect yourself and learn to survive the best way you know how but, unravel to trust the Father. Just know that He can help you if you allow Him to do so.

About The Author

Samantha Brett

Samantha Brett was born November 16, 1983 to her biological mother Rebecca Brett and father unknown. She is the older of two siblings. Her brother Tion Brett. She attended Granby High School and later received her Associates Degree in Social Sciences from TCC. Samantha has a passion for battered, bruised and broken women.

Chapter 9

Forgive Again

Forgive Again is for those who have found themselves in a familiar place that they never thought they would be in again. Especially, when you thought everything was going right and your life was finally coming back together again.

And you've gone through the necessary steps of deliverance, by forgiving all those involved including yourself, by praying and fasting, by putting God first, by reading more of the Word of God daily, by being held accountable and receiving godly counseling; while being restored. And because of the steps of deliverance, it caused the inner man within to become strengthened and you started living from that place, living from the inside out and now you're able to get back up and start pursuing life, the call and ministry again; without any unforgiveness in your heart.

But, then something happens and it's not anything new; but it's the same old thing you forgave them for the last time, but this time it's a hundred times worse than before. And you said in your heart, "I'll never let this happen to me again." But, here it is AGAIN months or years later hurt AGAIN; wounded AGAIN, crying AGAIN.

And you asked yourself why am I going through this AGAIN? Am I the only one? I just don't understand? I try to do what is right in the eyes of the Lord; but I find myself in this place AGAIN -- broken. I don't think I can take much more of this, my heart can't take it. "What about me? Lord, help me!"

But, this time was different from all the other times. It exposed the root cause of what's been hidden all these years, something from the very beginning; which now explains the depth of why this bondage kept coming back. You may have thought it, but you couldn't prove it until now. And now, it all makes sense to what's been going on; and some questions you may have had are now answered.

And now, you are finding out the truth of what's been going on. So, you try to stay positive! So, you can handle it the right way; but, then all of a sudden the memories start flooding your mind of what you went through before.

Then a fear of having to go back over the pain, torment, hurt, shame, rejection, unforgiveness, embarrassment, gossip and the looks. And you try to smile and keep doing the same things. So, that nobody will know and you start avoiding people and isolating yourself from everybody; while quietly slipping into a depression, because, you're trying to hold it all together for the sake of your family, friends, church family and those who may know your situation. You do this; so, no one will know what you're going through AGAIN.

But, you start battling with those old feelings of what you felt and now your emotions are all over the place, then you're crying uncontrollably; because you want the pain to go away and wanting to fight and get revenge on the person or persons because you know, now.

And these same people have been in your face, watched your Facebook posts, came to your place of worship, watching you from afar but, have been with you from the beginning, the betrayal you feel when you now know the truth.

The scripture says in John 8:32: *"And ye shall know the truth, and the truth shall make you free."*

Sometimes, the truth hurts and sometimes, you don't want to know the truth; because, we aren't ready for the truth. But, when Gods timing and season collides and it's time for TRUTH; it's nothing that we can do about it; because God has an ultimate plan in making us free. He'll use the good, bad and ugly to accomplish His will in the earth. And many times, we don't see it that way because we are focused on ourselves and what we are going through at that particular time.

But, God is omniscient (all-knowing), omnipresent (all –present/all-seeing), omnipotent (all- powerful), God knows what we are going through, nothing gets by Him and He's able to deliver you even when it happens to you AGAIN.

Scripture says in Psalm 34:19: *"Many are the afflictions of the righteous: but the LORD delivereth him out of them all."*

Even in knowing what God's Word is saying to us, we can find yourself going back and forth questioning yourself of what you did wrong and was "I not good enough?", "Was I not pretty enough?" and how dumb I must be to have forgiven them all those times.

And you keep replaying it over and over AGAIN in your mind because you just can't believe it's happening to you AGAIN and you're wondering if it's ever going to change or that this is the way it's always going to be.

I can testify to being in this same place in my life not long ago and I remember I was praying and crying out to the Lord and I heard the Spirit of the Lord say FORGIVE AGAIN. And I said WHAT, FORGIVE AGAIN! I couldn't believe what I was hearing FORGIVE AGAIN, those two words is not what I was expecting to hear at the time. I wanted to hear the Lord say something that favored me. But that didn't happen even though I was so hurt, mad, angry, ready fight, leave and fight some more.

But, I kept crying even more and talking to the Lord about those two words because I thought it must have been a mistake or God must not have known what was going on in my life. And HE SAID FORGIVE AGAIN and then He took me to this scripture. And I read it while, I was still crying.

Scripture: Matthew 18:21-22: *"Then came Peter to him, and said, Lord, how oft shall my brother sin against me, and I forgive him? till seven times? Jesus saith unto him, I say not unto thee, Until seven times: but, Until seventy times seven."*

This scripture right here lets me know that it was God's will for me to FORGIVE AGAIN and to not let unforgiveness get an advantage in my life AGAIN but, to FORGIVE in every area; where I had been hurt. But this time, I had to FORGIVE down to the root; so I had to really allow the Holy Spirit to lead me and guide me to and through those areas until I got to the root, the beginning of where it began.

And I realized then that God just didn't want me to just touch the surface but, He wanted me delivered and healed all the way through until the root. God showed His love for me and all those involved by exposing the root to set us free, that why I say it was different this time; because He had a bigger plan, much bigger than what I was going through. God wanted to bring restoration to the family, as a whole.

So, at that point that it was important for me to FORGIVE. And God didn't want me to go backwards and be in that same place I was in before that took control of my mind, emotions, will. It had my soul all wrapped up in unforgiveness that it affected my health. Plus, God knew what unforgiveness would do in a person life; if they chose not to forgive.

The scripture says in Matthew 6:14-15: "For if ye forgive

men their trespasses, your heavenly Father will also forgive you: But if ye forgive not men their trespasses, neither will your Father forgive your trespasses."

Luke 6:37: "Judge not, and ye shall not be judged: condemn: not, and ye shall not be condemned: forgive, and ye shall be forgiven:"

Mark 11:25-26: "And when ye stand praying, forgive, if ye have ought against any: that your Father also which is in heaven may forgive you your trespasses. But if ye do not forgive, neither will your Father which is in heaven forgive your trespasses."

Unforgiving (adjective) means:
1. not disposed to forgive or show mercy; unrelenting.
2. not allowing for mistakes, carelessness, or weakness: dictionary.com

Bible Summary. A simple definition of unforgiveness is "a grudge against someone who has offended you". Another definition of unforgiveness is not having the compassion to forgive. Unforgiveness is a sin that causes us to think and do evil things.
Access-Jesus.com

Matthew 18:23-35 is about a man having unforgiveness in his heart towards someone else but, he was forgiven of what he owed and how he was turned over to be tormented. It's simply not worth holding on to unforgiveness. Unforgiveness has consequences that comes with it. Choose to FORGIVE AND FORGIVE AGAIN.

The scripture says in Joshua 24:15: *"And if it seem evil unto you to serve the LORD, choose you this day whom ye will serve; whether the gods which your fathers served that were on the other side of the flood, or the gods of the Amorites, in whose land ye dwell: but as for me and my house, we will serve the LORD."*

Deuteronomy 30:19-20: *"I call heaven and earth to record this day against you, that I have set before you life and death blessing and cursing: therefore choose life, that both thou and thy seed may live: That thou mayest love the LORD thy God, and that thou mayest obey his voice, and that thou mayest cleave unto him: for he is thy life, and the length of thy days: that thou mayest dwell in the land which the LORD sware unto thy fathers, to Abraham, to Isaac, and to Jacob, to give them."*

So, when we look at forgiveness and why it is so important for us to FORGIVE in any situation and everybody it frees us the penalty and the consequences of it.

To FORGIVE means to cease to feel resentment against (an offender): pardon forgive one's enemies
> (a): to give up resentment of or claim to requital (see requital) for forgive an insult
> (b): to grant relief from payment of forgive a debt
> Webster-Merriam

Forgiveness means releasing the other person or people from blame, leaving whatever happened in God's hands, and moving on. And now you're not being controlled by the person or what happened to you. FORGIVENESS doesn't excuse what they did to you but it frees yourself and also you free that person and now your sins can be FORGIVEN. You've put FORGIVENESS into action and it's all working out for your good.

Now, FORGIVENESS is a process it is not to be rushed as bad as we want it to go away it's going to take time, but you must be willing to go through the process of FORGIVENESS.

Process means a usually fixed or ordered series of actions or events leading to a result   (Thesaurus-Webster Merriam).

So, allow the Holy Spirit to walk you through this process to bring deliverance, healing and restoration.

FORGIVENESS humbles you and put you in a position to help you accept what God is saying to you at that particular time. It puts your heart at God's ear to respond and move on your behalf; because you are now being obedient to the Word of God.

Isaiah 1:19: *"If ye be willing and obedient, ye shall eat the good of the land:"*

In Matthew 18:21-22, Peter asked the Lord, *"How many times should I forgive the brother who sinned against me, and Jesus said 7 times 70 and THAT'S 490 times."* But, God knew that we would mess up a lot in a 24 hour period and even though that's a lot to FORGIVE one person who repeatedly does the same thing we still must FORGIVE AGAIN because we never know when we will find ourselves in that same place time and time again and need that same person who caused you so much hurt and pain to FORGIVE when you fall short.

Scripture says in Romans 3:23: *"For all have sinned, and come short of the glory of God;"* We need that same grace and mercy extended towards one another.

Luke 6:36: *"Be ye therefore merciful, as your Father also is merciful."*

Let me say this AGAIN! Don't let the enemy, pain, hurt, doubt, revenge and people (or yourself); hold you hostage and keep you from obeying what the Word tells us to do as believers. When GOD has made a way of escape for us and that's to FORGIVE and FORGIVE AGAIN!

FORGIVENESS PRAYER

Heavenly Father, I come to you in the name of Jesus, I thank you for forgiving me for all of my sins and I choose to forgive and forgive again *for all the hurt, the pain, the disappointments which caused me to have a broken heart. I forgive ____ for ____ and release them to you Lord, that they can now be free and I forgive and release myself from all the hurtful things that happened to me and I decree and declare that I am forgiven and I am set free, in Jesus Name, Amen.*

About The Author

Apostle Tina M. Beatty

Apostle Tina M. Beatty is the Founder and Senior Pastor of King of Glory International Ministries and Lion of Judah International Ministries in Charleston, West Virginia.
She is anointed to teach and preach deliverance to the captives with power and authority throughout the United States as well as, internationally. Apostle Beatty is a wife and mother of four children and five grandchildren.

She has preached at conférences, retreats, revivals, churches, workshops, as well as, had conferences PrayerQuake, I Lived To Tell It Bootcamp "Diamond in the Rough" and especially "I LIVED TO TELL IT DELIVERANCE AND HEALING CONFERENCE", which was birthed through her getting delivered and being healed. She's not ashamed to tell her testimony and let the people know that whatever you've done or whatever was done to you, YOU CAN LIVE and LIVED TO TELL IT!

Revelation 12:11: "And they overcame him by the Blood of the Lamb and by the word of their testimony; and they loved not their lives unto the death."

She is an entrepreneur with several businesses, such as Nappy by Nature Salon, Strategic Life Coach Academy, The Apostle's Closet, TMBeatty Ministries Inc., King of Glory Apostolic Network, King of Glory Worldwide Ministries, Kingdom Leadership Academy, King of Glory Unlimited Travel, I Lived To Tell It, LLC.

Chapter 10

I Was in the Dark; Now I'm in The Light

    In August 2016, I traveled to Accra Ghana with the man of God, Bernard, for our sister in Christ (Tammy's) wedding. Upon arriving Prophet Kyle and Apostle Matt picked us up from the airport. Followed by taking us to where we would be staying. When we arrived dinner was prepared for us and it was delicious. After that, we met Sister Esther; we all stayed at the same place. The next evening Brother Bernard and I received a word from Prophet Kyle saying that when we return to the U.S. that our lives would never be the same, he also said that we were in expectancy of a shocking surprise. Bernard and I had no clue what was yet to come. Meanwhile, two days had passed and I begin to feel sick; I thought I caught a virus of some sort. My brother, Bernard and Apostle Matt took me to a nearby clinic to get checked for any virus, but the test came back negative. My symptoms were nausea fatigue and vomiting I couldn't understand what was wrong with me. I couldn't hold anything on my stomach, I was so frustrated. I had no clue as to what was going on with me. I kept telling my brother, Bernard, I was ready to return back home. He told me don't say that the Lord would've never allowed you to come if it wasn't His will. All, I could say behind that comment was Amen. My brother in Christ also, told me; "I (We) were there for a purpose and for me (us) to receive what you (we) have come there for!"

    Eventually, I calmed down and tried my best to focus on my purpose of being in Africa. I am thinking in my mind I'm sick very far away from home and away from my children this is crazy. The very next morning prophet Kyle knocked on the door of my room asking to speak with me privately I said yes, he said I know what's wrong with you I said you do? Prophet Kyle said your pregnant! I said what, how can this be? He said the Lord said, "That it is your heart's desire to conceive another child." I told the prophet this is true. It has been a prayer of mine to God to conceive again. I was perplexed at this point, after hearing such news. He then began to tell me that the Lord my God has place the seed of a child in my womb. Later that day, we went to have dinner with Bishop Paul. We arrived at the restaurant and Bishop Paul greeted me, he then asked me how I was feeling; I told him that I was feeling the same. He asked for the man of God Bernard to get him a bottle of water, so he could pray over it. Bishop prayed over the water and asked for me to drink it all. Within thirty- minutes, I had to run to the bathroom the water came back up. I couldn't get off my mind what prophet Kyle had told me earlier that day. I was still in disbelief, I then came out of the bathroom, and everyone had left out to the parking lot, I went where everyone else was at. When I got outside everyone asked, "Was I okay?" I replied, "No, the water came back up!" Bishop Paul came to me place his arm around me and said, "My daughter do you know why you are having these symptoms?" I said no, "Why?" He said, "You're pregnant!" He then asked me; do I want a boy or girl? He then laughed, out loud. He said, "I saw it in the spirit." I asked, "Are you speaking of future?" Bishop said, "No!"

    Now, I begin to ask God, "How can this be?" Later on that week, all that were participating in the wedding went to get our final clothes fitting. As I was trying my dress on the seamstress said, "My sister, it looks like you've picked up a little weight." The seamstress had to take the hem out to give me more room in my dress. It then dropped in my spirit here goes another sign of pregnancy. I was confused and had absolutely no understanding on what was going on with me. I began to pray to God asking him to give me confirmation on the word that was spoken over my life from the prophets. Meanwhile, Apostle Ernest flew in a day before the wedding from Nigeria. This was my first time meeting him in person. I had spoken to him several times over the phone; I met him through my sister, Esther. We were headed out from where we was staying and was on are way to a conference as we were walking to the car Apostle Ernest said, "Angel the spirit of the Lord just spoke and said you are pregnant!" Apostle Kyle placed his hand on my stomach and repeated three times, "Angel baby!" It happened so quickly before I realized, I lifted his hand off my stomach and Brother Bernard said out loud, "Why is he touching your stomach?" I told him, "I didn't know!" So, then he walked off being repelled to what just occurred.

Shortly, we made it to the house in complete silence. Everyone said good night and went to their rooms; while I and Brother Bernard went for a walk he asked, "Why would you allow for Apostle Kyle to touch your stomach like that?" I replied to him and said, "I moved his hand." Brother Bernard then said to me, "He had no business touching your stomach!" We went into prayer, gave it to the Lord and prayed for the peace God to remain and for God to be in the midst of us all. The next day it was time to say our good byes and go back to the U.S., before boarding our plane brother Bernard and I took lots of pictures with the men and women of God and thanked THEM for such great hospitality. Though, it was a very lengthy flight it was a blessing to visit Africa.

Finally, we made it back home safely, after being home for a few days those same symptoms of sickness came back. I tried my best not to think about it, but I began to have cravings for certain foods like pineapples, apples, pizza etc. It got to the point, if I didn't eat right away starting in the morning I began to get really bad headaches. The vomiting stopped, but the nausea still existed. I was so puzzled to the point; I went to get a pregnancy test. I took the test and it came back negative. At this point, I was still worried I couldn't understand why I was having those symptoms and the test was saying, I was pregnant. Now, I was at the point as to where I was ready to go to the doctor; even though I was still in denial I wanted to know what was going on with me. So, I went to the doctor where they gave me a pregnancy test and drew blood and both tests came back negative saying, I wasn't pregnant. So, I began to go to God and I ask Him, "Is this of Him and if I'm pregnant why isn't it showing on the pregnancy test?" I remembered with the pregnancy of my last child that it was different and several tests/blood drawn. And the doctors kept telling me that I wasn't pregnant; even on ultrasound it showed no signs of me being pregnant until almost six months. That's when I went back to the doctor for the last time and that's when I heard my daughter's heartbeat for the first time; I believed for this to be the same situation for me. So, I said I will wait a while longer to see if it was too soon for the doctors to detect the pregnancy. So, I did just that!

Weeks later, I noticed a bulge starting to form in my stomach and I was not too happy about my body changing at all. Soon after, I started a new job and I would be doing assistant living overnight staying at some of the clients' homes. This particular evening, I got my client settled in for bed and begin to worship and I was led to reach out to a man of God that I knew of in New York. When I called him, he told me he had been praying and fasting for one-week and that he was waiting on my call. He immediately began to declare over my life and we got off the phone. I begin to pray and thank God for everything He was doing in my life not even knowing what was ahead of me.

I went to lie down and right after that, maybe about an hour; after lying there I began to hear a voice. It appeared to me to be the voice of the Lord. At that time, He said to me, "My daughter, I'm doing work in your womb and I'm blessing your womb." As He was speaking to me, I felt a hand that appeared to be the hand of the Lord. I couldn't do anything but lay there. Thirty-minutes later, I began to feel nausea, hunger pains and tenderness of the breast. I then felt my back cave in -- I officially had an arch in my back and my stomach was experiencing changes. Hours later, I spoke to Apostle Ernest and he told me he saw the hand of God in my womb. I asked him, "Are you serious?" I thought I was losing my mind at first about what I actually just heard and felt in my womb. The man of God confirmed it all.

Eventually, I knew I would have to tell the man of God, Bernard, sooner than later. I just didn't know how to explain this to him when I couldn't make much sense of all of this myself. I eventually gained enough courage to sit him down and to tell him about everything. His first response was, "How could this be?" I told him I don't have any answer, but I'm going off my body changes and based off my previous pregnancies it's almost identical to them all. So, the man of God also suggested that I return back to the doctors. This time, he went with me as support. This time the doctors ordered various tests to see if this body change was all my imagination or me thinking I'm pregnant. And they also ran tests to see if there was any hormonal or thyroid gland issues. Every test they ran came back normal. The doctors could not explain why my body was changing, as if I was pregnant, they were all puzzled! I even went to have a second opinion with a specialty doctor and after she ran tests and given me an ultrasound; she told me maybe I miscarried and she then told me I was her "mystery" for the day. None of the doctors had answers for me nor could they explain why my belly began to get bigger and bigger. At this point, months later; I begin to experience movement and kicking so by me experiencing all of this I was convinced it was a baby in my womb I just was seeking God to ask him why the pregnancy wasn't being revealed. It took the man of God Bernard a while to receive this due to the fact my stomach was getting bigger by the month and I was weight gaining by two –to-three pounds a month. Apostle Ernest, Prophet Kyle and Bishop Paul would check on me on a monthly basis telling me to make sure I eat plenty of fruits and giving me instructions concerning the pregnancy. They told me the reason for the pregnancy not being revealed with doctors is because I was carrying a miracle pregnancy and that God didn't want the hands of man over the pregnancy.

Shortly, after the man of God drove me back to my hometown to ask my father for my hand in marriage, my parents were very pleased with him and gave their blessings. My family friends and co-workers wanted to give me a baby shower. So, the following month by the man of God, Bernard, who was known by my fiancé; along with my children hosted a baby shower for me. It was everything I desired. Eight-weeks passed and I suddenly begin to have actual Braxton Hicks contractions, which were on/off for about two-weeks. After making several trips to the doctors, with no success and no answers; we just begin to trust God and allowing the men of God that was in our life in that season to give us instructions for what we knew at the time was from the Lord. Suddenly, the pain stopped at this point I didn't know what to do, I had to even resign from my job; due to me having severe back issues. One day, my fiancé's mutual friend of ours came to do a conference in Minnesota, Prophet Jordan. We went to see him and we explained to him what's been going on with me. And he said, "Let me pray about it, but he said I will say this, "It's nothing to worry about and I'm not sensing anything bad." I was a little relieved but not 100 percent.

Now, a whole year has passed and I'm still in this condition and my fiancé and I decided to relocate to Texas. So, in the process I started having issues with my stomach staying firm and would shrink and then weeks later it would come back full and firm; I was a nervous wreck. I wanted to make sure that my unborn child was okay. I would go to God asking Him, "Why am I going through this way?" If this is of you, "Why do I feel like I'm suffering?" I would cry out to God, as often as, I could. It was having my fiancé feeling stressed and very bothered by seeing me in this condition for well over a year. We finally got settled in Texas and we began to attend Prophet Jordan's church in Dallas. By this time, I picked up extreme weight I begin to not feel or look like myself, I quietly slipped into depression. I cried every day and I felt alone. I felt like no one could understand what I was facing. Even, in the mist of me praying to the Lord, my fiancé and I would have different men of God come to us asking to sow a sacrificial seed for the babies to come to pass. My fiancé and I were asked by Prophet Shawn to raise a seed of 400 dollars; so, he could buy spiritual candles and the babies would be released. He said he saw two people (a man and a woman) at the river; they cracked an egg over the water to bring me harm. He also said he would first need to go to the cemetery to reverse the curse. And shortly, after he does the instruction; I can deliver my babies.

Now, I entered into a new year; family members upset and angry, because they spent their money and brought baby items and still no baby or babies. I truly couldn't tell them anything because I didn't know what was going with me. At this point, neighbors, associates and family stopped talking to me and were publicly talking about me. My own sister was going around telling other family members, "I'm crazy, I'm pregnant; but haven't delivered the babies yet!" It was a lot going on but through all this and trying to plan a wedding it was a lot. It was God that kept my head above water. The day before my wedding, I received a phone call from my cousin, Yavette that I hardly talk to; she began to plead with me asking me not to marry the man of God placed in my life. She couldn't even give an explanation for her calling with that foolery. The wedding proceeded on July 21st, according to God's plan. The enemy tried to creep in, but we defeated the devil that day. There was a slight delay with the pastor that was marrying us; his flight was delayed, due to the weather. But God turned everything around for my good; the wedding ceremony and reception was everything I asked God for.

One month into our marriage, I was led to reach out to my brother, Apostle Tyler. I began to explain to him my situation and his exact words were I heard the Lord say, "It has to be a woman!" Apostle told me he wasn't going to connect me with anyone, he was going to connect me with someone that I was going to see the power of God manifest. He gave the woman of God my contact information and she reached out to me almost immediately. She asked me to tell what's been going on and how could she be of any help to me. As I begin to explain to her, she said let me stop you right there! She said, "That's not of God and God don't operate like that, it doesn't take one-year for God to bring a baby to pass. It only takes nine-months for a woman to conceive/carry a child!" She said you need to go through deliverance. I then asked the woman of God if I can go get my husband. So, he can hear everything and gain understanding on what has taken place with me. She then began to explain what took place with me and that it was very demonic and that I was illegally violated. She explained to my husband and I (both) that the attack was against the marriage taking place (for it not to come to pass).

A few weeks after our wedding, I received a phone call from my son telling me my father had passed August 8th; all I could do is cry but I knew I had to be strong for my children. I called the man of God, who is now my new husband, to give him the bad news about his father-in-law. We made plans to travel to Chicago to attend my father's homegoing. At the time of his passing, things weren't planned out in unity as my father wished. So, I just remained quiet; but very observant, until we departed for our return back to Texas.

About The Author

Angel (Kirklin) Harris

My Name is Angel (Kirklin) Harris I am from a small town called Phoenix, IL. My parents are Albert and Doris Kirklin. I am the second child of three girls: Shenea, Kirklain (eldest sister) and my youngest sister, Karla Kirklin. I am currently married to Christopher Harris. I am a mother and a grandmother of three children Jalyn, Asja, Allaya, Jalyn has a daughter her name is Hunter. I received Christ as my Lord and Savior at an early age. My church home is Danielle Chapel of Zion located in Phoenix, IL.

The Lord has called me to a healing and deliverance ministry – that is in the birthing process. God has given me the passion and the ability to work with the youth and in the healthcare industry; to love, care/nurture and healing the sick. I currently have a degree in Early Child Development and I will be attending school for my Bachelors of Science in Nursing Degree.

Chapter 11

Once, I Was Able to Exhale

As I prepared to pen this chapter, many things came to mind and into a manifested state. The excitement was quite evident once given the news of the opportunity to share my experiences on this topic, but then something else occurred, as well… Stay tuned!

Life has its way of happening to all of us. Our experiences vary, yet we share similar times that can be similar. This is how it works when we go through the various stages within our blessed, yet eventful lives. So, we must be ready to take upon each moment as it comes and do our best to look upon it with a positive perspective. In my years of life, I have seen and experienced many things; however in this Chapter 11 of 12, I am going to deal with getting to the point of doing something that many have faced or will face in their own life.

According to Merriam-Webster, exhale is defined as the process of breathing out. But what do you do, when breathing is the underlining issue of difficulty? This question was one that was posed to me personally in more ways than in a natural sense, but in a spiritual or supernatural one. I have discovered a great parallel as it relates to both. In life, many things happen that causes this to occur. An individual may never understand what the next individual may encounter or face; however, we can say with certainty that challenges have been present. My time of awaiting the exhaling state appeared to be a process that just seemed to become longer and more complex than I ever wanted to experience. It came to a point that I just wanted to see some signs of change occurring.

The overall process reminds me of the time in my life where I experienced difficulty within a medical diagnosis that related to breathing. There are many definitions for breathing, according to Merriam-Webster; it is defined as:

1) (a): to draw air into and expel it from the lungs: RESPIRE broadly: to take in oxygen and give out carbon dioxide through natural processes (b): to inhale and exhale freely 2): to blow softly 3): LIVE 4): to pause and rest before continuing 5): to feel free of restraint.

I was in a time in my life where just taking a normal breath was quite tedious and sometimes heart-wrenching to those that were in my immediate circle. My parents and siblings were there to experience their bundle of joy as a daughter and baby sister born with a list of possible challenges, according to "man" or natural doctors understanding of the case. But from the eyes of God, I was already an OVERCOMER and VICTORIOUS! And because of this, I was not limited in any form or fashion.

However, that was an example within my stages of development and I was blessed to be showered with love, encouragement and a strong support system. In addition to, possessing that child-like faith that we often hear about in many spiritual settings. My reality was placed before me as no limits and the reports of the medical professionals were respected, yet not received as the LAST SAY! So, now that I am classified as an adult or "all grown-up", what's NEXT? ... Let's Continue...

The word once denotes that it has "happened or occurred in the past: formerly." So, the process of being able to exhale has now taken a new meaning. I am no longer looking at it as just being able to do the act of "breathing out", but realizing that this is attainable; because it has been done before. No longer do I look at the situation as one that is something that is unconquerable; but with the blessed assurance that my time of exhaling is nigh. And this provides consolation and comfort during times of weariness. There is such a calmness and peace that surrounds and blankets you when you come into this realization.

Many times, the cares of life become a weight; rather than an accountability piece. Simply put, according to Merriam-Webster, weight is defined in these ways: a: something heavy: LOAD, b: a heavy object to hold or press something down or to counterbalance: BURDEN, PRESSURE. This reminds me of the scripture in Hebrews 12:1 – *"Wherefore seeing we also are compassed about with so great a cloud of witnesses, let us lay aside every weight, and the sin which doth so easily beset us, and let us run with patience the race that is set before us,"* There is such a great parallel within this passage because "weight" is mentioned, as well as, sin. However, they are distinctly separated and are not the same; which is a vital component of understanding how this can affect any individual at various times and in many forms.

Now, that more light has been shed on the overall process; it's time for a more in-depth experience through my eyes. Join ME… The opportunity to embark on this awesome writing project presented itself and as I stated earlier; excitement was definitely one of the feelings that was felt by me. It feels so good when you know you are walking on a path that is set for you by God. As Psalm 37:23 states, *"The steps of a good man are ordered by the LORD: and he delighteth in his way."* This is how I felt at the time of the invitation being presented and I had no hesitation regarding my decision of acceptance; but with acceptance, came responsibility. I am reminded of Luke 12:48, *"But he that knew not, and did commit things worthy of stripes, shall be beaten with few stripes. For unto whomsoever much is given, of him shall be much required: and to whom men have committed much, of him they will ask the more."* I was like "Aha!" This has taken a new meaning, despite how many times I had heard the scripture previously. My very own invitation to pen this very chapter has revealed a deeper plan than what I ever though or imagined. Jeremiah 29:11 states: *"For I know the thoughts that I think toward you, saith the LORD, thoughts of peace, and not of evil, to give you an expected end."* Wow, I am walking through this experience and not realizing that an important life-changing lesson was unfolding before my eyes. This definitely was shifting my thinking from a natural (carnal: worldly) view of the situation and transformed into the supernatural view of God's plan for me. *"And be not conformed to this world: but be ye transformed by the renewing of your mind, that ye may prove what is that good, and acceptable, and perfect, will of God."* (Romans 12:2)

In the meanwhile, life is happening with its diverse factors with it; which means no day is the same. So, this is the part that is integrating the accountability piece that was previously mentioned. And what is accountability? Accountability is defined as an obligation or willingness to accept responsibility or to account for one's actions (Merriam-Webster). This word is one that many have heard, used, but oftentimes have not chosen to adopt into practice. However, this does not take away the true essence of what it means. I can say personally that many times in life, we use the fact that we are "weighted down" with so much that this gives us a pass on the accountability piece in our own lives. And yes, weight does affect us in ways that can lead to non-production; which confirms that it is being used as an excuse. This allows me now to proceed into the exhaling process... Let's Go a Little Further...

We have now come to the awaited time of "exhaling." Life is happening as it will do, no matter whom or where you are as it relates to it. The victorious testimony from my own childhood was mentioned earlier to assist in painting the picture to now. And it was something that comes to me in my present day. It allows me to stay focused and grounded in what I have faced, shall face and what's to come. It provides time to pause and reflect on all that I may be experiencing and that is the very moment that I can prepare for the comeback. Someone may ask, "What is this 'comeback'?" I am so glad that you asked. Let Me Elaborate... The entire chapter up to this point has been preparing you for being able to understand the "exhaling" process. And now, the awaited time of "breathing out" seems as a more realistic next step. As the title of the book is BREATHE AGAIN, we must come to this point or we will expire (to breathe one's last breath: DIE – Source: Merriam- Webster Dictionary). Realizing further that you can die both naturally and spiritually. This allows me to reflect on John 10:10 – *"The thief cometh not, but for to steal, and to kill, and to destroy: I am come that they might have life, and that they might have it more abundantly."* This is what it has been about the entire time. There is a constant plot against those that are possessors of value. A thief has a specific plan of action towards the one that is seen as possessing something that is desired. So, now that this has been brought completely into the light; not hidden – What's Next? ...

Psalm 118:17 states, *"I shall not die, but live, and declare the works of the LORD."* My time of feeling like there was a hindrance, hesitation or obstruction in my breathing was under my control. I had been given authority from the Most High to command my entire body, situation, life and all that encompassed it to come in Divine alignment. All of the life events that were happening were just that! As we oftentimes may hear the common phrase, "life happens!" And again, indeed it does; but our perspective towards it is what determines the outcome.

I AM determined that no level of challenge is enough for me to give up. Yes, we will face those times that it may cross your mind to "throw in the towel"; but it should not be an option for you. Remember, that even in the very face of the "thief" that you SHALL LIVE! *"For God hath not given us the spirit of fear; but of power, and of love, and of a sound mind."* (2 Timothy 1:7) *"And the LORD God formed man of the dust of the ground, and breathed into his nostrils the breath of life; and man became a living soul.* (Genesis 2:7)

"...Be Empowered and Allow the Breath of God to Overtake You -- Like Never Before!"
– Dr. MGM –

About The Author

Dr. Mia G. McGee

This multi-faceted woman of God serves in many capacities in the Kingdom. She utilizes the gifts that God has given her through business, education, and ministry. Her principles and concepts are all based on God's Word and her successes in these areas are because of the anointing and favor that has been placed upon her by God. As an Entrepreneur, she uses her knowledge, gifts and abilities to help other realize and activate their purpose. And in business, she can be found using her own success as CEO of AHP Consulting & Business Solutions, LLC; President of W.A.V.E. Outreach Ministries and Independent Learning Partner/Online Liaison of Vision Virtual Learning to encourage others to follow their dreams in pursuing their educational/professional goals.

Dr. Mia G. McGee was called & Chosen at a young age, this woman of God serves in the 5-fold ministry apostolically & prophetically. Mia walks in the office of a prophet(ess) of God and does not mind telling you what "thus saith the Lord". She is the daughter of Charlie Grice, sister of Elvis Grice and Jacqueline McClinton. And holds the honor of being a devoted wife to Corrie; mother of Corrie (Jr.), and Angel, along with being a spiritual mother to many. She cherishes to memory mother, Ethel M. Grice and her first-born son, Devan.

God not only gave her a "vision" for W.A.V.E. Ministries Inc., where she is the CEO/President. She also serves or has served in various leadership capacities, including: Founding Pastor/ Overseer, Associate Minister, Youth Counselor, Armourbearer, Ministry Assistant, Choir Member and many other giftings in the Body of Christ. Dr. McGee is an Affiliate of Woman of God Ministries International and serves as Executive Assistant to the Founder of Bridge International Missions, under the Leadership and Spiritual Covering of Apostle Trena Stephenson.

Mia has been featured on many platforms, speaks worldwide and serves as an editor and columnist for various newspapers, books and magazines. And has been featured as a host and guest on many local and national radio & television networks/stations, throughout the country and abroad. She holds many degrees/credentials, and wears many "hats", including an Adjunct Professor for various colleges/universities.

Dr. McGee often states, "What degrees and/or credentials I hold is not relevant to the anointing that I possess from God. Yes, I thank God for them, but since you may want to know, I did receive a Ph.D. (Prophetic, Healing, Deliverance) from the University of the Holy Ghost, located in the Holies of Holy, the Heavenlies, all these exceed any earthly letter."

Contact Information:

Mia G. McGee, Ph.D.
Website: www.MiaMcGee.com
1-877-406-0730
Email: Booking@MiaMcGee.com
appointed for the Kingdom of God.

Chapter 12

Breathe Again....
Just Breathe

    One hot day in June 2017, I was going about my day as usual. I had no complaints everything was going great in my personal life and ministry. Well, the day had turned into night and I decided to look at my passport, which was held in a security box that houses all my personal documents. I only went in it to confirm that my passport was still valid. I had an upcoming international mission trip coming up. Well, as I was looking for it I ran across some documents that forever changed my world as I knew. I discovered a very serious breakdown in my family. Something that I knew would cause a huge shakeup. What do you do when you have to choose between loyalty and truth? Especially, when that person meant the world to you what do you do? I choose truth it was the hardest thing to do, because it involved someone who I considered to be the closest to. (Psalm 25:5 – NKJV) *"Lead me in Your truth and teach me, For You are the God of my salvation; On You I wait all the day."* Someone, I looked up to and sought consistent approval off.

    I measured my success to there's and felt that if I was half the person they were, I would be doing good. But what I perceived was right wasn't and what I perceived to be truth wasn't. It rocked my world and shook my very foundation. I looked up to them personally and in ministry. Deception is tricky; I found out loyalty creates blindness. Things I discovered were done over several years of my life undetected at least by me. I called my brother and cried on the phone because I was in so much shock. My heart was broken and I felt my breath had left my body. After my call ended with my brother, I prayed and cried myself to sleep. I was questioning everything God was anything real what I saw displayed before me as an example was it all fake (Romans 16:17-18 (NKJV) *"Now I urge you, brethren, note those who cause divisions and offenses, contrary to the doctrine which you learned, and avoid them. For those who are such do not serve our Lord [a]Jesus Christ, but their own belly, and by smooth words and flattering speech deceive the hearts of the simple)."*

See, I grew up in a preacher's household; all I knew was church. And to see the breakdown that happened in my family was devastating. No one really knew, but a few, as to what was going on. I found myself losing my breath, literally. I began suffering from anxiety, which I never had experienced before. But, I felt lost and really didn't know what to think and do with the news of what I discovered. I didn't share it for many months, because I knew it was going to forever change what I saw as a dependable foundation for me. God asked me, *"Who are you going to obey, me or your fears?"* (Jeremiah 7:23 - NKJV) *"But this is what I commanded them, saying, 'Obey My voice, and I will be your God, and you shall be My people. And walk in all the ways that I have commanded you, that it may be well with you')."* I said God I choose you. It's easy to say I'll choose God no matter what until you're faced with the realty of losing a relationship with someone you hold very dear to your heart. My yes was painful I knew the storm was going to be great ahead of me but I knew God was going to get me through. Once I revealed what I found; everything around me seemed like it was crumbling in my personal life. Ministry was great, but my personal life in complete shambles.

What do you do when things crumble around you due to your stance for righteous? (Deuteronomy 25:1- NKJV) *"If there is a dispute between men, and they come to [a]court, that the judges may judge them, and they justify the righteous and condemn the wicked,.."* I'll tell you STAND in spite of. In spite of, the venom now spewed to you from the very one you adored. It was once crushing blow after the next. But, I kept praying and was not in denial of my pain. I kept battling lack of sleep and now anxiety. Blessings of the Lord falling simultaneously in the midst of my life storm. When I reflect back today, I know it was God encouraging me that I had done the right thing. But, I will be honest my faith was so shook because I began to question everything that I was taught by this family member; because I began to see they weren't living up to what was taught to me. My emotions were all over the place concerning this situation. How can you say one thing live another? Not only had that hurt someone that they said they would always love. I didn't understand it…Yes, I know I am an Apostle! And you may say, "How could she think that?" But keep in mind, an Apostle is my kingdom assigned place.

But, I'm still human and suffer like anyone else. Many times, I feel it's even greater; because I lead. But, I held on to my belief that God would not put on me more than what I could bear. Time continues on I'm still in the thick of the life storm. I was still very much confused as to why this had happen. I said God please let me know why me and why am I facing this storm which I consider the greatest storm I have faced in life to date. God said to me, I had to show you that the only sure foundation you should believe and stand on is me alone (

> Matthew 7:24-27 (NKJV) "Therefore whoever hears these sayings of Mine, and does them, I will liken him to a wise man who built his house on the rock: and the rain descended, the floods came, and the winds blew and beat on that house; and it did not fall, for it was founded on the rock. "But everyone who hears these sayings of Mine, and does not do them, will be like a foolish man who built his house on the sand: and the rain descended, the floods came, and the winds blew and beat on that house; and it fell. And great was its fall."

I was like "WOW! God, I thought I was." He said you weren't fully because if you were you wouldn't have been so devastated. I began to repent immediately asked God for forgiveness (Acts 3:19 (NKJV) " *Repent therefore and be converted, that your sins may be blotted out, so that times of refreshing may come from the presence of the Lord.*" After that moment, I began to look at things differently. I began to have compassion concerning the family member. I began to reflect on their life journey at least what I had knowledge of, and said to myself something has to be broken somewhere to make the decisions they made. I began to see that I had placed them on a pedestal that they didn't even ask to be placed upon. It's nothing wrong with esteeming others but be careful that you don't idolize them because if you do you are about to be greatly disappointed no of us is perfect.

    I truly believe as bad as it was no one really knows the mind and heart of a person but God. I had to stop trying to diagnosis the satiation trying to find a way to understand. I finally began to turn it completely over to God (Psalm 55:22 (NKJV) *"Cast your burden on the LORD, And He shall sustain you; He shall never permit the righteous to be [a]moved.)."* Do my part, but allow God to cover the areas I couldn't. And at that moment, my breath returned and anxiety began to lift (1 Peter 5:7 - NKJV) *"casting all your care upon Him, for He cares for you.)."* I found a way to be in peace in the midst of the chaos (Philippians 4:7 - NKJV) *"and the peace of God, which surpasses all understanding, will guard your hearts and minds through Christ Jesus".* Did the storm cease? No, but my perspective changed. I had a renewed strength to endure

    (Isaiah 40:3 (NKJV*) "The voice of one crying in the wilderness: 'Prepare the way of the LORD; Make straight [a]in the desert A highway for our God'."*

See, what many don't know is that anxiety shifts your breathing pattern; as my breathing began to become normal again in the physically. I started to see and feel the breath of God spiritually in a whole another way (Job 32:8 - NKJV) *"But there is a spirit in man, And the breath of the Almighty gives him understanding."* I began to see that God wanted an exchange for me giving over total control and letting him control, without conditions. See, if you would be honest when life situations arise you serve differently. Webster's dictionary defines breathe as to inhale and exhale freely. If you are not careful when going through life storms; you will encounter breathe blockers. Unforgiveness, fear and lack of faith just to name a few. I was in the midst of one of my greatest storms and I encountered breathe blockers. I had to fight through every single one. It was tough, but it was a must. Don't let the storm stop you from breathing. I was struggling, until I got my breakthrough. God had to shift my upset and disappointment to compassion.

When I began to take my focus off of them and place it upon myself, I began to see there were areas in me that needed to be fined tuned. Think of it this way, you can have a vehicle that runs very smoothly without breakdowns or failures. However, a tune-up is still required to maintain the longevity and good continual performance of the vehicle. So, even though I walk in love and compassion; I can always do better. It wasn't until I felt my breath failing me that I realized I was due for a spiritual tune up (Isaiah 41:10 - NKJV) *"Fear not, for I am with you; Be not dismayed, for I am your God. I will strengthen you, Yes, I will help you, I will uphold you with My righteous right hand."* I'm so grateful that God brought it to my attention, before it was too late. People of God, just because you look and seem well; doesn't mean you are completely well. Storms come to better us not to overtake us. If you feel overtaken that means you have encountered a breath blocker and you need to address it. So, you can move forward.

As God continued to deal with me it became easier and easier to breathe. My trust and dependency on God took a whole another meaning, God, I can't breathe without you! There is no way I'm coming out of this if you don't breathe on me and my situation (Jeremiah 30:17 - NKJV) *"For I will restore health to you and heal you of your wounds,' says the LORD, 'Because they called you an outcast saying: "This is Zion; No one seeks her.'"* God began to release to me instructions on how to navigate this storm I found myself in. Believe or not God put me on mute. Don't speak nothing just let me BREATHE. See the breath of God can resuscitate something that is dying or dead. I began to see the hand of God move upon me like never before. My heart and compassion has expanded through this storm. I learned the only perfect one is God himself. No one determines my end but HIM (Deuteronomy 32:39 –NKJV) *"Now see that I, even I, am He, And there is no God besides Me; I kill and I make alive; I wound and I heal; Nor is there any who can deliver from My hand"*. Just breathe…blow out fear and breathe in faith. Blow out anger and breathe in forgiveness. The breath of God is vital for us; we can't do anything unless, HE breathes. God breathing on me and my situation is what changed things around. It brought my focus back and instead of talking about the problems I call it the "woe it's me syndrome." I began to seek the face of God for solutions. I want you to know, I am the better because of the storm. I have a better appreciation for life and God. The spiritual tune-up was much needed, it showed me I got to do better and be better. If it's not life-giving, accept the divide God allows. I realized I didn't need what I thought I needed, my validation and approval only comes from God (Galatians 1:10-12 (NKJV) 10 "For do I now persuade men, or God? Or do I seek to please men? For if I still pleased men, I would not be a bondservant of Christ.11 But I make known to you, brethren, that the gospel which was preached by me is not according to man. 12 For I neither received it from man, nor was I taught it, but it came through the revelation of Jesus Christ". But, sometimes when its family; we don't hold ourselves to it, we make exceptions. No one family or otherwise should impact your stand and relationship with God. I removed that family member off the pedestal within my life. Only God reigns supreme. It's a good feeling when God breathes, I needed to be restored and replenished and only the breath of God can do that.

  Man will always fail you, but God will never fail us, as long as, we acknowledge we need him (Luke 1:37 – NKJV) *"For with God nothing will be impossible."* I didn't even realize until the storm hit that my breath was diminishing. People of God the enemy is trying to take the very breathe out of you (John 10:10 - NKJV) *"The thief does not come except to steal, and to kill, and to destroy. I have come that they may have life, and that they may have it more abundantly."* Having us fall in the midst of the storm, instead of standing and waiting to see the salvation of the Lord. Life is teaching me that my breath will fail me, but the breath of God will sustain me. Allow God to breathe again…allow him to restore your will power and stamina you can make it. Don't allow the enemy to make you feel that you can't get past what your current situation may be. Learn while you're in the storm and recognize those hidden truths that God shows you about you.

Take your eyes off of others and place them upon yourself. See them as a troubled soul, not an enemy. Love them through it, even if you have to do it from a distance. The breath of God comes to restore every area that is dead. Let the breath of God consume every area of your life, if you could have fixed it; it would have already been done. I made it out of the storm stronger and better than I was when I went in. I learned that I could only control what I do and how I respond to others or the situation that arises in my life. I learned I'm not the fixer, God is. The only way to survive is to allow the sustainable breath of God to breathe on me and my life storms. I'm so grateful for what God is doing for me and through me. Has the broken relationship been restored? Not yet, but I believe God will bring forth totally restoration. God is still yet breathing on the situation. You stay focused on what is assigned to your hands continue to breathe remain in peace, until you see the manifestation of that thing.

Say this prayer with me,

God forgive me of anything that I have done knowingly and unknowingly to upset you. I am coming to you with a repentant heart. My breath has failed me; I need you to breathe on me again and my situation. Allow me to see it the way you see. I will be forever grateful I pray this prayer in Jesus name! Amen and Amen.

About The Author

Apostle Trena Stephenson

Apostle Trena Stephenson is a woman of Excellency, Inspiration, and Compassion. She believes in empowering others by speaking truth that comes from the unadulterated Word of God.

Apostle Stephenson was ordained as an Elder through Bible-way Churches of America Worldwide, under the Presiding Prelate and Chief Apostle Cornelius Showell. And in December 2010, Apostle Stephenson was elevated to the office of Overseer of Woman of God, Inc.

In May 2019, under the leading of the Lord, Apostle Stephenson united with Dominion International Ministries, Apostle Dr. Yolanda Powell and Pastor William Powell as her spiritual covering. Apostle Stephenson serves as a mentor to diverse groups of women from various denominations and backgrounds. She also serves as Founder and Presiding Prelate of Bridge of Hope Deliverance Ministries & Fellowship of Churches, which currently provides oversight to several ministries nationally/internationally.

Apostle Stephenson has been afforded many ministry opportunities/ speaking engagements to travel throughout the United States, as well as overseas, in locations such as: Africa, Poland, Paris, Israel Jamaica and various cities in Germany.

Another component to the ministry of Apostle Stephenson is the radio/ television broadcasting and programming. She has been featured as a special guest on these broadcasts: "The Wenda Royster Show," a radio broadcast of Radio One; Rejoice TV Network; TBN (Trinity Broadcasting Network), and Preach the Word Network. Not only has Apostle Stephenson been interviewed on shows, she has been the interviewer. In April 2008, Apostle Stephenson became the Executive

Daughters of Distinction / Breathe Again

Producer and Creative Director for Daughters of Distinction TV, which housed two shows; Daughters of Distinction Live and Let's Talk.

Apostle Stephenson's unconventional ways to relate and touch God's children in all walks of life has been what makes her ministry unique. This can be seen by Apostle Stephenson's mounting passion and expertise for writing and helping others. As a result, Daughters of Distinction (DOD) LLC, was birthed in 2008. And in 2010, under the DOD umbrella, Apostle Stephenson launched Soar Magazine, an online publication to empower and encourage the people of God. This has been yet another publishing ministry that Apostle Stephenson has been able to share with others, as well as, her platform to highlight other ministry leaders, writers, psalmists, artists and authors for the edifying of His Kingdom. She has authored and compiled several books and has produced a number of titles under the book publishing component of DOD.

Lastly, to find out more information about the ministry, media and/or messages from this powerful woman of God please visit these websites: www.wofgod.org, www.dofdllc.com, http://bridgeinternationalmissions.org, http://www.blingbyapostlet.com and www.dailylivingnetwork.net

Apostle Trena Stephenson is a "Participating Voice"
in the upcoming documentary film & media training materials about
'Apostolic Women in Leadership Worldwide'

Bonus ....

Bonus Chapter

JUNIA ARISE

Shining Historic Light On the 1st Woman Apostle

In Romans 16:7, the Apostle Paul writes with strong commendation about Andronicus and Junia, who were relatives that served as apostolic leaders in the 1st Century Church. He refers to the duo as "outstanding among the apostles." Andronicus was male. Junia female. Most biblical scholars believe they were married and both apostles.

Today, this biblical insight is still a disturbing controversy among many church leaders and male preachers who refuse to accept the reality of female leadership in the Kingdom. Yet, the overwhelming evidence among most Greek scholars and many theologians now emphatically conclude, that Junia was the FIRST WOMAN APOSTLE.

As Apostle Axel Sippach, leader of the EPIC Global Network writes, "There are countless pages you can find online with experts undeniably proving this from the Greek. Those opposed are really in the minority now. For 700+ years Junia was the "lost apostle." The lost first "WOMAN" apostle. This conspiracy and religious cover-up have now been exposed."

Ironically, it appears that most Believers & Followers of 'The Way' were aware of Apostle Junia for the first 1200 years of church history. Then around 1300AD Bible translators began to use the male form "Junias" instead of the female "Junia." Adding the "s" essentially transgendered Junia and ultimately made her a male apostle in most versions of the bible for over 700 years until recent time.

"But Junia was a popular name within Roman culture 2000 years ago and was vastly used in differing forms of literature. However, the male version, Junias (Junius) is not found in contemporary 1st century Roman or Greek literature at all. So, with expert validation, this biblically old coverup and conspiracy has lost its credibility," as Apostle Sippach writes. Yes! The devil tried it, but his schemes and plots to keep this important woman out of biblical history has utterly failed. We now know who she is and what she represents...The liberation of women worldwide – both in the church and in culture!

So, we rejoice that Apostle Junia is no longer a "hidden figure" buried in the archives of Holy Writ. During the summer of 2018, the EPIC Global Network in tandem with Dominion International Ministries held the 1st Historic & Congressional Summit called, Junia Arise: Apostolic Women on the Frontlines and was able to veto the error and reenact the law of God concerning the woman. It was a massive legislative convening.

During that Summit, the 'Key of Junia' was prophetically released in the Nation's Capital that unlocked the multiple gates were women were held bound and imprisoned—from government and business to media and religion. Ironically, this was done in "The Year of the Woman" as the both violations and victories experienced by women globally hit the nightly news. A new epoch for women's empowerment was massively forming throughout the earth and the life of Junia was at the forefront of change.

Honestly, where would the church be without faithful women of God? Like Junia, we have always been on the frontlines and in the trenches getting the work done—in service, prayer, hospitality, teaching, discipleship, evangelism, missions and much, much more.

So Junia really is the GAME CHANGER, as THE FIRST WOMAN APOSTLE! And this factual truth heralds the important positioning of women in leadership at the highest levels of Kingdom Government and at every helm imaginable throughout the world. It validates and vindicates the woman in extraordinary ways and soundly repositions her as a vital member in the eternal plans of God Most High.

Next spring 2020, we will bring Junia Arise: Shining Historic Light on the 1st Women to the big screen as a documentary film across all seven continents. It's time to tell her story, so that women all over the world can be free from male-dominated misogyny and be liberated to serve our King with boundless energy, expertise and empowerment. To become a Junia Champion and support this great effort go to: JuniaArise2020.com

****

Dr. Yolanda Powell is the visionary leader of Dominion International Ministries & Worldwide Companies and the Executive Producer of Dominion Films based just outside Washington, DC. She is a Marketplace Apostle with a prolific call to the 7 Mountains of Cultural Influence. To learn more about her ministry visit: www.yolandapowell.com

Releases from Daughters of Distinction

He Still Hears

He Still Speaks

He Still Sees

He Still Waits

7 Ingrediants

www.ingramcontent.com/pod-product-compliance
Lightning Source LLC
Chambersburg PA
CBHW070516100426
42743CB00010B/1840